I0759269

THE FIRST 33

One Woman's Journey
From Trash to Treasure

Part II
The Untamable Teenage Years

Bridgett LaRé

This book is dedicated to all the Powerful Kings and Phenomenal Queens who are suffering in silence. Some may feel inconspicuous, voiceless or estranged due to overwhelming pressures imposed by society. You are not alone; the good news is... there is hope! I have been there and can assure you that it will get better. The world sees you. The world hears you. The world needs you. Receive it! Believe it! Achieve it!

Love,

Your Sister Friend, Bridgett LaRé

Table of Contents

Executive Editor: LaDeya Ivy

Introduction

In the untamable teenage years, God was there for me in more ways than one as I flirted with addiction, self-hate and death. There was no light shining from my existence, yet God's grace and mercy was there for me through it all. This book is a transparent, raw and unconcealed depiction of those times.

You may be wondering why one may feel compelled to share their journey for the world to see and why you should read it. Well, I believe the enemy's triplets; shame, embarrassment and guilt, are a sure way to keep us in bondage. They hinder us from healing of past injustices and living the abundant life that Jesus came to earth for us to live. I share my story to relinquish the power of "the triplets" and to encourage you to do the same.

In order to heal from the past, you must sit with it and feel it. Talk about it, write about it, scream about it, punch a pillow about it; whatever you must do to release those pent-up feelings and emotions. As you boldly share your story with others, you are unconsciously a source of courage for them to share their own story and begin their healing process.

Although this book is filled with juicy, colorful and exciting adventures, I encourage you to notice God's grace, patience and merciful hand of protection, while I made numerous beautiful mistakes as most teenagers do. What I label "beautiful mistakes" are the times we make decisions that are not in our best interest, nonetheless, we learned a lesson and gained knowledge, wisdom and understanding because of it.

If you ever felt hopeless, lost, misguided or invisible, then this book is for you. I'm hoping my truth will provide you with the comfort of knowing that you are not alone. We are never really alone; God is always here with us and for us.

In my teenage years, I felt like I was trash and therefore treated myself as such. Can you relate? If so, I'm here to tell you from experience that the struggles you've endured will build your strength. YOU ARE TREASURE. You may have been buried in some mess but you were always treasure. Some of us are required to dig a little deeper than most to uncover our jewel of a self. This book series is in essence a collection of truths about my treasure hunt and I hope it encourages you to seek, recognize or share yours.

"The thief does not come except to steal, and to kill, and to destroy. I have come that they may have life, and that they may have it more abundantly." -John 10:10 NKJV

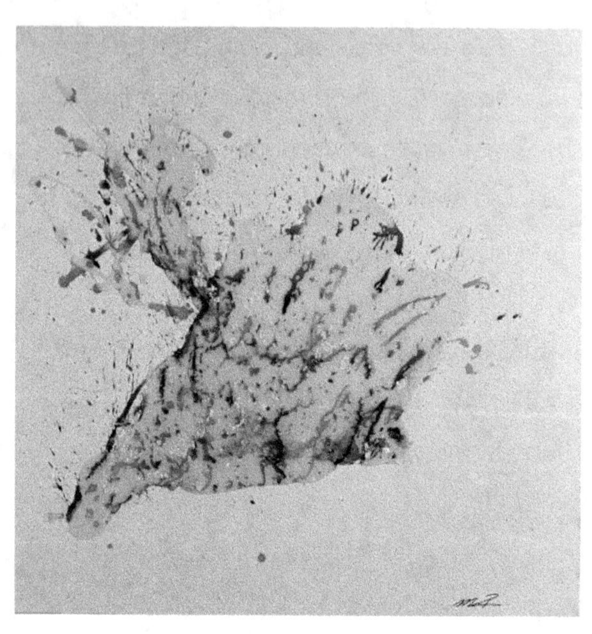

Mike Angel Reynoso Perspective Art
"Changing Your Perspective"
Los Angeles, CA

Chapter 1: Roll Up

It's imperative that this book starts off with the biggest lesson of my teenage years. One that took me 20 years to comprehend and I'll never forget. Picture this...I'm 13 years old, pretending to be asleep in bed around midnight. With the blanket pulled over my head, I found comfort in the dark abyss that was metaphorically paralleled to my dark existence and way of being. It also muffled the boisterous lawnmower sound that kept me tossing and turning on most nights. "Einnnnnnnnn, Einnnnnnnnn, Einnnnnnnnn," the sound continued as I waited for my beeper to vibrate. (If you were born after the 90's, just ask Siri or Alexa what a beeper is!).

The lawnmower sounding noise was actually my mama's sleep apneic snoring, indicating she was knocked out deeply enough for me to sneak out of the room without alarming her. My mama, sister Deya and I shared a room in my grandparents' home. They lived in a small ranch styled yellow brick house centered right across the street from one of the most infamous projects in Dayton, Ohio.

Finally, the beeper softly vibrated. It read, "800-911-304". Since pagers were only numerical, my friends and I were creative in turning numbers into words. I deciphered the message from my homegirl Brianna that lived across the street in the projects. 800 looked like Boo, which is my nickname, 911 is the American number for emergencies and 304 spelled the word "hoe" when you turned the pager upside down. Brianna's message said, "Boo, it's an emergency Hoe!" That indicated my boyfriend Darius and his friends were outside with all our party favors like Seagram's Gin & Juice, marijuana and Newport cigarettes.

After spider crawling over Mama to get out of bed, the escape plan was in motion. Slipping on my Stivers Middle School sweatshirt, some jeans, and sneakers, I tiptoed down the hallway past my grandparents' room. Per usual, their door was shut so there was no worry about them catching me. I continued to creep down the carpeted hallway, smiling, dancing and thinking, "Yes! I haven't smoked all day and I can't wait to see my baby!"

Upon approaching the kitchen, which was the way to quietly get out of the house, I noticed that the light was still on but gave it no further thought. I kept creeping, smiling and dancing as I walked into the kitchen and was blindsided by the presence of Papaw quietly sitting at the table with his legs crossed. Have you ever been caught in the act of doing something wrong? Do you remember how you handled yourself? Psychologists say that our acute stress response is to either to fight or flight. I froze!

"Oh my God!" I gasped, releasing a sudden short intake of breath. Papaw looked up at me and then continued checking his diabetic blood sugar while remaining silent. Being that I was accustomed to receiving butt whooping's by Mama, I instantly assumed he was about to tear me up for trying to sneak out of the house! Papaw calmly stood up, walked to the refrigerator, poured himself a glass of orange juice, slowly drank it for what seemed like five minutes and then finally began to speak.

"I remember when I was your age. I used to be outdoors a lot because I had to be outdoors. See, we lived in a small house on a farm in Carrollton, Georgia where there was no plumbing. We used to have to go outdoors and use the outhouse." I couldn't even begin to imagine using a wooden potty outside and wiping my butt with a leaf. Could you? Papaw took another sip of his orange juice and continued. "I used to have to go outside and chase down hogs, drag em' to the house and chop em' up so we could have food on the table." I was standing there grossed out and gagging under my breath, picturing Papaw being all barbaric and killing his food himself. I wondered if he enjoyed performing the mechanics of the task, but I didn't dare ask being that I was awaiting my inevitable beat down.

This was the first time I actually saw him as a human that grew up to be a grandfather and not just the old man I'd always known him to be. Me as a 13-year-old kid was starting to feel sorry for his 13 year old self. A part of me still wanted to bolt out of the kitchen door and over to the projects to be with my nocturnal compadres. Another part was highly intrigued by the stories Papaw was sharing and wanted to hear more. I didn't know he had to go through all of that.

"I even had to go outside to pitch water from the well to drink and bathe in. Y'all kids got it so easy these days. If you want water to drink, all you have to do is go to the refrigerator and get it. If you want food, you can go to the refrigerator and make a sandwich. But for some reason y'all kids like to run these streets doing only God knows what." Papaw gulped down the remainder of his orange juice, put the cup in the sink, walked over to me and gently placed his hand on my shoulder. "I'll tell you what, if you want to go outside and fend for yourself, then you go right on ahead. Otherwise grab a snack from that refrigerator and gone' back down yonder to bed now, ya hear?" He then walked to their bedroom and shut the door.

Papaw gave me permission to run the streets and be ratchet but I didn't know what to do at this point. I had never been prompted to make a decision for myself before. There was a dilemma, should I roll up on Brianna in the projects and make some beautiful mistakes tonight or not? Unfortunately, for my party girl spirit, Papaw's stories and loving concern left me feeling all warm, vulnerable and domesticated.

I poured myself a glass of orange juice, sat down at the kitchen table and called Brianna. "Bitch, my grandpa done caught my ass. I ain't gon' make it tonight. I'll get up with you at school tomorrow." Going back down yonder to the bedroom, I quietly crept in bed, pulled the blanket over my head and fell asleep for real this time. That isn't to say that I didn't go on living a bad girl lifestyle which you'll read about in these pages, but on that particular night, the right decision was made to prove to Papaw, myself and essentially Mama that I was capable of being responsible without getting a whooping.

My family wasn't the mushy, touchy-feely, "I love you", type of family and Papaw taught me that wasn't the only way to love. It took 20 years, but I learned from him that a lot of times love is an action. He showed love by the action of storytelling and he did it so well that it rubbed off on me. My message to you is to be like Papaw. DO (action word) love in whichever way you feel is most authentic to you. Writing this book series and transparently sharing my life story is my way of loving you right now as you read this sentence. I encourage you to figure out how those closest to you DO their loving and genuinely appreciate them for it.

A year after Papaw left that lasting impression on me, Grandma Jewel's death left unfamiliar feelings and emotions that I didn't know how to express. Not wanting anyone to see me cry, I hid in the bathroom to grieve the loss of our family's matriarch. She died on the national day of love, Valentine's Day. That holiday made the list of occasions we covertly agreed to not celebrate in our household. Once Grandma passed, I got back to the basics and began sneaking out of the house at night again.

My beeper kept beeping, "911-911-911!" It was Brianna and she's never done that before. I successfully snuck out of the kitchen door expecting the worse. Amidst the grassy field, drug dealers and addicts on the street corner, there stood my friend Brianna. I scanned the scenery, pondering what the triple 911 emergency could be. There was a small group of uncanny teenage girls cursing loudly amongst one another. They were looking towards Brianna as she frantically jumped up and down, waving her arms in the air, motioning for me to come her way. Immediately, I suspected drama. It looked like we could beat them up so I wanted drama.

She must have gotten into an argument with those girls and needed me to help her fight. That was my rationale. With high doses of adrenaline gushing through my veins, I ran over to Brianna who was now scavenging through her purse. Assuming she was looking for her razor blade to fight unfairly, I pulled the silver box cutter out of my sweater pocket, edged it up to expose the blade and whispered, "What's up Bitch, we got drama?"

"Nah girl! That's my neighbor and her friends talking about a fight they had at school. They cool." She pulled out a quarter pound bag of marijuana from her purse and threw it at me.

"Where the hell did you get this from?" We both knew she didn't have a job or money to pay for anything more than going half on a dime ($10) bag.

"You know Daddy always gives me what I want." She stuck her tongue out and seductively gyrated her pelvis in a slow grinding motion.

Daddy is what she called her boyfriend Ricky who was about 20 years our senior. Many boys our age were attracted to Brianna but she preferred the older men. She was short in stature with caramel skin, a pretty face, sassy mouth and what men described as the body of a grown woman.

"Tell Daddy I said thank you!" I picked her up off the ground and twirled her around in celebration of the big score.

"Tell him yourself. Let's go sit on his porch and smoke." Brianna opened up the door to her apartment and yelled, "Grandma I'm spending the night at Ricky's. Watch little man for me."

"You know I don't like you messing with that grown man!" Her grandma worried. Ricky had his own apartment in the same complex where they lived. Although we were the same age, Brianna didn't have to sneak out like me. She had a baby with her ex-boyfriend and was treated like an adult.

Ricky was sure to provide drama once we got to his porch. He didn't care for me and the feeling was mutual. He had an issue with Brianna hanging out with my 15-year-old boyfriend Darius and his "horny little friends", as he called them. He was smoking a Newport, looking at me in dismay as we approached him. Remembering that he supplied us with the weed in my pocket, I plastered a phony smile on my face. "Hey Ricky, good looking out on the trees!" He didn't respond.

"Roll up Hoe!" Brianna handed me a grape Swisher Sweet Cigar then jumped onto Ricky's lap. Eager to smoke, I sat on the steps and focused on crushing the marijuana buds into small particles.

"Boo!" Someone yelled. "What you doing out here without letting me know?" I recognized my boyfriend's voice and physique as he galloped towards me in the darkness. I licked the cigar, split it open and gutted the tobacco out into the grass, contemplating my response. He was with a couple of his "horny little friends", so I knew Ricky was going to be disgusted by their presence.

"Hey Babe," was all I could come up with when he made his way to the porch. Then I sprinkled a nice amount of weed into the cigar and rolled it up.

"Who invited y'all over here?" Just as anticipated, Ricky was being petty.

"This my girl, I don't need an invitation old man." Darius was not intimidated.

"You and your little boy band don't want these problems homeboy." Ricky threatened. Brianna covered his mouth pleading for him to be quiet. I lit the blunt, passed it to Darius and demanded he and his friends walk me home.

Over time, the tension between the two of them grew stronger. I was convinced their issue went deeper than Ricky disapproving of Darius and his friends being associated with Brianna. No longer did they react with verbal threats or violent outburst. Mutual death stares seemed to suffice. The dislike they shared for one another began to pour into Brianna and my friendship and we drifted apart.

Darius and I were inseparable but our relationship consisted primarily of skipping school at his place, smoking weed and drinking alcohol while he played video games. After a few months of our boyfriend/girlfriend child's play, he concluded that it was high time for us to take things to the next level. Walking his mountain bike alongside us while escorting me home one day, he presented me with the inevitable.

"Nobody at your house right?" He questioned.

"Not for another hour or so. Why what's up?" I stopped walking and looked at him suspiciously.

"You know what's up. It's my way or the highway!" He had a seriousness in his eyes that reeked of frustration.

"What do you mean?" The clenched teeth and nervous smile indicated that no further explanation was really needed.

"Either we do the nasty today or we break up today. What's it going to be Boo? My way or the highway?" He reiterated.

Other than being violated at the irreproachable age of 9, I hadn't allowed a boy to know me in that way and wasn't interested. "It's going to be the highway then." I grievously murmured while staring into the windows of his soul, searching for comfort.

"Alright, your lost!" He geared up onto his mountain bike and disappeared into the intricate maze of the projects.

A few months passed without us seeing one another. He was missed but not contacted because I wasn't willing to give him what he wanted. My feelings of pleasure and gratitude came from drinking alcohol and smoking weed. Nothing more and nothing less.

One wretched day, Darius's mother called to inform me that he'd been shot and killed at someone's apartment in their complex. An overwhelming feeling of devastation, guilt and doom washed over my body. Knowing about his history with Ricky, my gut feeling told me that he had something to do with it. I convinced myself that if we had never met then this would not have happened. The guilt was invalid but real. I extended my condolences and promised his mom that I'd attend the funeral.

Without hesitation, I went to the streets to get a definitive answer as to what went down. According to the neighborhood gossip, Darius was at home playing video games when he received a phone call from an unknown source telling him to come outside. Moments later, he was found lying in a pool of his own blood, clinging to Ricky's kitchen floor with nothing on but his birthday suit penetrated with bullet holes.

Not knowing if Brianna and Ricky were still a couple or not, I immediately called to see if she heard about the heartbreaking news. "What's up?" Brianna answered in a dry and irritated tone.

"Girl! Do you still mess with Ricky? Have you seen the news? Did you hear that he killed Darius?" The questions spewed out of my mouth, nauseated with sympathy, hurt and concern.

"I heard it was something like that, but I don't know for sure. I got to call you back though, my Grandma getting on my nerves." She suspiciously replied in a cold manner and then hung up the phone.

"What the hell?" Was Brianna the friend that made the phone call to lure Darius out of his apartment and into his demise? Did she and Ricky set him up together? Why was she acting so distant and apathetic? Talking with Brianna left me even more flabbergasted than before.

Continuing with the investigation, I contacted one of Darius's "horny little friends". Allegedly, Ricky called the police after he and his girlfriend woke up to an intruder breaking in. He voiced to the operator that they better get there soon because he had a gun and was prepared to use it. The police informed him that help was on the way and to stay upstairs. When the police arrived, they discovered the gruesome murder scene.

Due to Ricky's phone call, the detectives obviously rationed one interpretation from the deadly attack. Self-defense. He was not charged or sentenced for what I suspected to have been premeditated murder. Although Darius's friends and family expressed their concerns, it was an open and closed case without further investigation as far as I know.

Brianna and my friendship dissipated without further discussion. As far as I was concerned, she was guilty by association at the least. I decided to keep my distance from her, Ricky and the projects.

Mama sat by my side at Darius's funeral. I kept my head held high enough to hold back the grief-stricken tears and remained strong. She could not see me cry. It was a sign of weakness where we came from. I resolved to internalize the hurt by doing what I knew to do best; numb with marijuana and booze to escape the pain of reality.

A few weeks after Darius's funeral, some girls and I were skipping school in the downtown Dayton area. As we crossed the intersection of Third and Main Street, there was Ricky sitting at the red light, watching me with a scowl. Our eyes locked as I stopped in the intersection and suddenly had the urge to urinate. Just like when Papaw caught me trying to sneak out that night, I froze in fear and instantly forgot how to put one foot in front of the other. The girls were too busy chatting it up to notice the trio was missing one.

Ricky's eyes were a blurry portal of nothingness and his mouth grinned with satisfaction. He bent down and slowly lifted his hand as if he were pulling a gun from under the seat. "Should I scream, duck, run or crawl?" I scrambled my brain to make sense of what was going on. "He's either about to shoot me on the spot or throw me in the back of that van and torture me!" That was the only rationale I could conjure up in my 14-year-old brain. Just then, one of the girls realized my absence from the trio and yelled for me to catch up.

Snapping out of the trance, I continued to walk across the intersection with my eye's laser focused on Ricky, anticipating an attack. He inched his hand out of the window and I braced myself for the impact of a bullet. He laughed hysterically while waving his middle finger in the air. The light turned green then he stuck his tongue out and swung it from side to side as he sped through the intersection, missing me by an inch. I skipped a short distance to avoid his attempt to side swipe me, jumped on the sidewalk and ran to catch up with the girls who were none the wiser.

With a murderer on the loose that had it out for me, I sought after a new boyfriend who was fearless enough to kill for me if it came down to it. The qualifications for my new and oblivious bodyguard were to have easy access to money, marijuana and guns.

Shortly after my revelation, Sarah, a friend of the family moved into the projects across from my grandparents' house. She was a beautiful single mother of one, in her early 20's, who didn't look nor act her age. The sweet aroma of Jasmine body mist preceded her entrance into any room. She walked with confidence in her 5'10" slim frame, long legs and hefty bust which she highlighted with all the latest teen fashion.

Sarah was very friendly with men and they flocked to her like bees looking to pollinate her flower. Her baby boy had the cutest little green eyes with curly hair and the most contagious laugh I'd ever heard. Incentively, he loved to slobber people with his loving hugs and kisses. I needed them.

Visiting Sarah and her baby was the first time I'd been back to the projects since Darius and I broke up. I stood on the patio with the baby on my hip, smoking a blunt and reminiscing about Darius. My day dreaming was interrupted as a tall, slender and dark chocolate figure approached me. "So, Bridgett got a baby now?" He joked with a voice deep enough to penetrate the marrow in my breastbone. It was none other than the handsome Cole, one of Darius "horny little friends".

"This is my friend's baby. Boy you know I ain't got no kids." I playfully whispered in a tone soft and seductive enough to get paid $1 a minute as a late-night phone operator.

"You know Ricky left the hood, right?" He informed me.

"Good cause I thought I was going to need a big strong man like you to keep me safe. His crazy ass was stalking me." The sound of those words coming out of my mouth for the first time was chilling.

"That punk already know I'm on the lookout for him for what he did to my boy. Plus, I always had a crush on you so you ain't gotta worry about him. I got your back." He hurled his voice with conviction, representing the protection I was looking for. Seeing Cole again sparked the kind of attraction that connected the missing link to my marijuana addiction.

He quickly became my new boyfriend, bodyguard and weed supplier who made sure all of my cravings were fed. Babysitting for Sarah while she hung out at night was the perfect plan to see Cole. A few months into our relationship, He and I were getting wasted with Sarah and listening to music. Feeling the vibes, we began passionately making out on the couch. "Y'all need to take that upstairs." She interrupted.

"Hell yeah! Let's go upstairs!" Cole eagerly agreed to her suggestion.

Unlike Darius, he never pressured me for sex and I didn't give it a second thought until Sarah encouraged me. In her bedroom, we exchanged physical and spiritual DNA with every bead of sweat dripping from his bare body and onto mine. He held and secured me down with his light body weight and tickled my ear with, "I love you's" and other sweet dialogue. The feeling was explosive.

Was this the love and protection that I'd been so desperately searching for? The body high equally numbed and heightened my vulnerabilities even more than weed did. I could feel another addiction coming along. After he plateaued to the point of climax and I didn't, Cole withdrew his manhood which was missing the protection we amateurly placed onto him as a team.

"Oh my God! Where is it?" I whispered in a panic. He carefully performed a digital exam of my cervix, dislodging the empty condom from inside. We discussed what we would do if I were indeed pregnant. Cole said he would do whatever to take care of me and the baby. Outside of selling drugs, I couldn't envision what he meant by that. Grandma Jewel always warned me, "Your fast ass better not bring any babies home for me to raise!" Although she had passed, Mama wouldn't be too pleased either.

When my monthly flow arrived indicating that I was not with child, a newfound appreciation for freedom was born. The pregnancy scare made me realize that I didn't want any attachments, including Cole. When we first got together, I was vulnerable, seeking refuge from Ricky and grieving the loss of Darius. He was a convenient, safe and willing participant. After a few months, I broke it off with him and my unlimited supply of free marijuana.

Did you know that a common escape to numb the pain associated with trauma is the use of drugs, alcohol, food or sex excessively and irresponsibly? All of which can be very addicting, troublesome and even deadly. Have you had trauma in your life that may be causing you to struggle with any of these issues? Could you use an unbiased listening ear and practical tools to better yourself? If the answer is yes to either of these questions, the good news is...There is Hope! I highly encourage you to seek professional help from a therapist, life coach or spiritual leader. All three have played a pivotal role in my healing process once I let go of the stigma behind seeking help.

Maybe you've been telling yourself that you can change anytime you want, but you just don't want to right now. Maybe you're looking for a sign from God that you need to pivot. Whatever your reason is behind doing the things that no longer serve you, I'm here to tell you that this is your sign! The fact that you picked up this book and are reading this sentence right now is your sign. Seek help today, not tomorrow. Remember what Dr. Martin

Luther King, Jr. said, *"The time is always right to do what is right!"*

"When you pass through the waters, I will be with you; and when you pass through the rivers, they will not sweep over you. When you walk through the fire, you will not be burned; the flames will not set you ablaze."
Isaiah 43:2 NIV

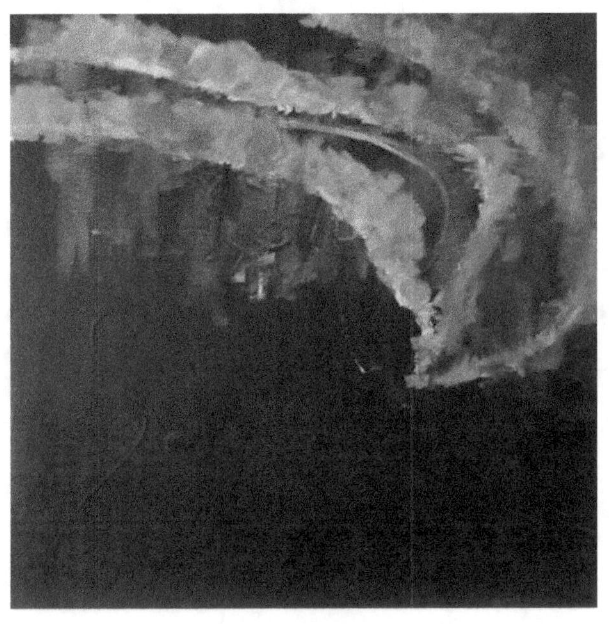

Art by Amani Ivy

"Northern Ocean Lights"

Dayton, OH

Chapter 2: In The Heat Of The Night

Skipping school only to hang out at different schools and pretend to be a student there made no sense but it was fun to me. One day I decided to visit my cousin DeNora at Dunbar High School. That's when I met Eric. He brushed past me in the hallway, causing my beeper to fall on the floor. "Excuse you ugly!" Being sassy was my superpower.

"Ugly? You don't even go to this school. Why are you here?" He picked my beeper up, inspected it for damage and handed it to me. "Here. It didn't break."

"You lucky! I'm just dropping something off to my cousin but it's none of your business anyway!" I snatched my beeper from his hand.

"Liar. You're always up here skipping school, but I won't turn you in for truancy if you give me your number." He smiled revealing his pearly white teeth and kind eyes.

Scanning Eric from head to toe in order to identify any areas of interest, I weighed his pros and cons. He was much shorter than I liked my boyfriends, but he was slim, handsome and chocolate like Cole. His ears poked out like they were trying to escape from his face but it was kind of cute. On top of everything, he appreciated my sassy mouth and bad attitude.

"Alright Mr. Goody Two Shoes! I'm only giving this to you so you don't snitch." I lightened up and gave him my beeper number realizing he'd bumped into me on purpose.

Eric didn't drink or smoke and constantly nagged on me about going to class like a good girl. My favorite comeback was, "That's how you met me!" Although I appreciated his loving concern and our witty banter, being with him was monotonous as compared with Darius and Cole. I decided to spice things up a bit.

Home alone one night, I enticed Eric to hop on the RTA bus to come over. Without even saying hello, we kissed passionately as soon as he stepped in the door. We found our way in Papaw's room and onto his bed. I was gratified in knowing that my good guy was being a bad boy with me. The mere excitement of us getting caught sent surges of electrical currents throughout my body.

Eric touched me in places he had never touched before and intensified the pulsations in sync with my heartbeat. Papaw's door suddenly swung open, demanding our attention. Mama barged in with a frantic look of astonishment.

"Ms. Donella!" Eric shrieked.

"What in the hell y'all in here doing?" Mama turned the light on and snatched the blanket off of us.

"Uh," was the only word that I could think of.

"Get the hell out of here boy!" Mama grabbed Eric by the ears and showed him the way out the door.

"I'll call you later!" I awkwardly shrilled, foreseeing the beating she was about to put on me. Surprisingly, Mama instructed me to take a bath and go to bed. After eagerly calling Eric so we could laugh together about getting busted, I was dumbfounded when he broke up with me. He stated that he shouldn't have gotten involved with a girl of my caliber in the first place.

Have you ever had someone say something that stung you to the core? Something that you held on to and continued to play over and over in your head? For a long time, a low caliber girl rang in my ears, earning a place in my subconscious. It took many years of self-work to stop believing what other people said about me and start owning what God says. God says we are a royal priesthood. Don't ever forget that. Even in your darkest hour, believe that you will soon be called into the light because at your core, you are Royalty!

Mama eventually met a man of her own, the infamous Keith. The first time we interacted was in my grandparents' driveway one night. He got out of the car and began talking like we were familiar friends. "Well look at you looking just like your Mama! I know this is your baby girl right here Donella!"

"Uh...Mama, who is this?" She shot me a look that reminded me to keep my manners.

"I'm the man that's taking care of her. She moving in with me for a while. I'll get a house big enough for all of us soon." He spoke with a deep, raspy and authoritative tone, not giving Mama a chance to speak for herself.

Refusing to acknowledge him, I looked at Mama for confirmation. "Is this true? We don't even know this man!" By that time, she looked like she wanted to pop me in my mouth, so I stopped talking to hear what she had to say for herself.

"Yes. Y'all going to stay with your Aunt Icy for a while until Keith gets a house for us." Her demeanor was softened and submissive. I'd never seen her act this way before. It seemed like he made her happy, so I forfeited the fight.

"Ok well, nice to meet you Keith." He extended his hand, I shook it and then went into the house to tell my brother and sister, Reggie and Deya who were as shocked as I was.

Mama soon moved in with Keith while Deya and I went to live with Aunt Icy and her five kids in the projects on the east side of Dayton. My brother Reggie stayed on the west side with our Uncle Avery. It was going to be nothing but trouble with my best cousin DeNora and I living together.

The two of us spent many nights hanging outside with the neighborhood kids until the break of dawn as they supplied drug addicts with whatever they were selling. I learned a lot about supply, demand, buying and trading from watching them make a living the best way they knew how. We were sometimes rewarded with jewelry from the dealers when the addicts would trade their family members stolen, sentimental possessions for dope.

As long as we were outside on the green thing (what we called the raised electrical unit that was within the projects) or on the porch where Aunt Icy could see us, she didn't have a problem with us being out late at night. We used to sneak and go to nightclubs often but didn't get caught until we tested our luck one night, which proved to be a horrible mistake. DeNora spent the night with her boyfriend and I stayed with some grown man I met at The City Lights Club the night before.

The next morning, I woke up with a pounding headache, nauseous stomach and numerous missed pages from Mama, DeNora and Aunt Icy. DeNora paged me from her boyfriend's number with 911 at the end. I knew it was nothing but trouble. Using the random dudes phone, I called DeNora to see what was going on.

"Girl my mama called your mama and told her we didn't come home last night. Auntie Donnie done called the police and reported us missing!" She frantically notified me.

"Oh my God! Get up! You have to take me home right now!" I shouted and elbowed the stranger beside me.

"What's going on and why are you on my phone?" He inquired, rubbing the sleep out of his eyes.

"It's my cousin! She said my mama called the police and they looking for me. You have to take me home right now!"

"I bet like hell I don't. I do not need the police questioning me, all up in my business!" Dude was not happy with me and my drama.

I'm not sure what warranted that response but it's likely he was on the run for something or fearful of being charged with statutory rape of a minor. Apparently, he wasn't going to help me out of the mess I'd gotten myself into. DeNora and I devised a plan to convince our mom's we'd spent the night over one of her girlfriends house. We were happy with our plan and decided to meet at the corner store.

The man dropped me off and that proved to be the last time I ever saw or heard from him again. DeNora's boyfriend dropped her off and we used the store's pay phone to call the police. That seemed like a better option than calling our mom's. We informed the police that we had been reported missing but that was all a misunderstanding, and we were headed back home now. They ordered us to stay where we were, and they'd send a squad car to pick us up and escort us home. "Good!" I thought. "Surely Mama wouldn't whoop me if the police were involved."

We arrived at Aunt Icy's place and the two officers walked us to the door. My mama swung the door open and greeted DeNora and I with fierce eyes and pursed lips. "Take y'all black asses upstairs and wait for me!" DeNora ran to Aunt Icy's room where she felt protected under her mother's arms. I stood by the stairway, eavesdropping on Mama's conversation with the police officers.

When I heard the woman officer tell Mama that she should beat our asses, it dawned on me that they weren't there to protect or serve us, neither did they care to. Since Mama lived with Keith, it had been a long time since I had a whooping. The memories sent me to DeNora's room to curl up under the blanket in a fetal position, anticipating what was to come. The officers left and the sound of Mama's footsteps creeping up the stairs sent aches and pain throughout my body.

"Donnie about to get y'all!" Aunt Icy warned.

"Don't let her whoop me Mama!" DeNora begged.

My mama opened the door to DeNora's room where I was, revealing the black leather belt that she'd apparently carried for such a time like this. I was clenching the blankets that were strategically wrapped around my body for cushion. "You better take them covers off!" She ordered with a strike of the belt, reminding me of what I'd been missing. Had I remembered, I probably would have thought twice before staying out all night. My cries were echoed by DeNora's screaming from the other room, imploring her mama to save her.

Once she was done being the judge, jury, prosecutor and executor of my case, Mama made her way to Aunt Icy's room to serve DeNora her sentence. I sobbed in silence nursing my wounds and listened as the leather belt made contact with DeNora's skin. The sound reminded me of the old western television show I would watch with Papaw, "In The Heat Of The Night". When the cowboys would whip their horses to get them to obey their commands. It grew to be satisfying listening to DeNora get a spanking. I was envious that she was often able to act out in ways that I didn't without consequences and repercussions.

Do you find yourself secretly hoping for the demise of others or being a hater as some would call it? If you can relate, I encourage you to examine yourself for the root cause of your issue. Once you know the foundation, you can build from there to free yourself of any negative emotions. After holding many invalid grudges for up to 33 years, I recognized that envy was a major weakness. Awareness was the first step towards a positive change in that area.

That incident put a stop to my street life for the moment. At least until I could find a way to do so without sounding an alarm. To my surprise, that way would be provided for me by none other than Mama herself! Her niece Nalena got a new job and needed someone to babysit her six boys while she worked the night shift. Mama, being a family orientated woman, volunteered Deya and I to babysit while we were on summer break from school.

Nalena lived on the west side of Dayton, right where I loved to be. She had a nice sized four bedroom house with a finished basement and lots of space for me to perform my bad girl activities without being on any adults radar. I eagerly agreed to be the new babysitter for my little cousins. Deya agreed as well but I doubt if she had any sinister intentions like I did. Her biggest incentive was that Nalena paid us in food stamps so she could buy all the Flamin' Hot Cheetos and Faygo Red Pop that she wanted!

Deya and I made quick friends with the neighborhood kids who helped us to care for the six boys. We spent a lot of time sitting on the front porch drinking, smoking and clowning around (except Deya). If we weren't doing that, we were walking up and down the streets, going from one person's house to the other, doing the same thing.

A couple of friends and I were chilling on Nalena's porch one day when GioVanni Price, my neighborhood crush, walked by. We frequently made googly eyes at one another but neither of us had the courage to say anything more than, "hello". I liked that he portrayed himself to be the quiet and shy type. From my experience, those were the boys who had something menacing up their sleeve and that brought out the lioness in me.

The white t-shirt was plastered snugly onto GioVanni's brown shoulders, arms and torso. He looked like a beautiful snowcapped mountain walking down the street. His tall stature stood strongly like well defined boulders of rocks that made up a mountain. His teeth were aligned, clean and pure like a virgin. GioVanni and his brother were walking home from the corner store when he gleamed at me and donned a smile. "How you doing Miss Lady?"

"Well do you really want to know or is that just a formality?" I replied in a sultry note and soft face.

"That's a real question that I'd like to come on that porch and get the answer to." He bit back.

"Come get it then." Gesturing towards my friends, "They were just leaving."

We sat on the porch getting to know one another until he then had to go home at sunset to meet curfew. That day led to us spending consecutive days together at either Nalena's house or his. His mom was very strict with him and his brother which prevented me from contaminating his character. He was an honor roll student that didn't drink, smoke or hang out in the streets. Having GioVanni as a boyfriend began to make a positive impact on my life. I began to go to class so he could be proud of me for being a good girl. I grew to be so infatuated with him that I'd rather spend countless hours being serenaded on the phone than running around in the streets at night, performing hoodrat antics.

A couple of months into our relationship, GioVanni and I were aching to get to know one another in a biblical sense. His mom and brother were always at home and we weren't allowed to shut the door while in his room. It was impossible to "do it" there. Nalena's house was usually crowded with family members and friends. We couldn't find the time to "do it" there either. Positive that Deya would give a report to Mama if she literally caught me with my pants down, I knew we couldn't "do it" if she was anywhere close to the vicinity.

One breezy summer night, I babysat the boys by myself while Deya was at her friends place, leaving me with a perfect opportunity to be alone with GioVanni. The kids were put to bed earlier than usual and I turned on some soft music to play in the background. I knew it was going to take some finessing to get him to break curfew.

"What's up Boo?" He answered the phone with a low, raspy, crackling voice, confirming my decision to be a bad girl that night.

"Come see me Baby. We haven't seen each other in hours!" My low and sexy tone matched his.

"You know my mama don't play that. Where everybody at though?" He questioned.

"My sister is gone and the boys are asleep. I'm just sitting here all alone, listening to this soft music and thinking about you."

"Oh I see what you trying to do! You trying to get us in trouble! You really want me to come?" He said with a bad boy demeanor.

"You said it, not me!" A devious grin was plastered on my face, knowing he was all in.

"I'm on my way!" He confirmed in a soft whisper then hung up the phone.

GioVanni's favorite mixed tape with all the 90's R&B hit music was playing on the boom box when he arrived. With a bright Kool-Aid smile and short of breath, he lightly knocked on the door so as to not wake up the kids. "Did you run to me Baby?" I mocked.

Standing in the foyer, heavily breathing, he pulled my body close to his and encapsulated me inside of his huge masculine arms while showering me with warm, passionate kisses and tender touches. Karyn White's song, "I Rather Be Alone" blasted through the speakers. GioVanni pressed his plump lips to my ear and sang along with Karyn...

"I won't be a fool, a fool for love, cause I know I rather be alone than be here unhappy."

His singing voice was heavenly. The low rumble from the bass in his vocal expression of love traveled through my ear canal and penetrated deep down into my soul. I wiggled around in anticipation, pinned up against the wall, willing and ready to give myself to him. In the height of the intensity of our foreplay, the front door creaked open sending the two of us into the attention stance of army soldiers.

We heard a voice call out, "Bridgett, what are you doing in here with all the lights off playing this slow booty call music?" Nalena had come home earlier than expected. There wasn't any time for GioVanni to hide in the basement or run out of the back door. Nalena walked right into the foyer and caught us drunk with passion, clinging onto one another and unable to formulate a good lie.

"Oh, this what you up in here doing! I see you got you a fine one too Cousin!" She acknowledged. "It's alright with me but you know Donella won't be ok with her baby cupcakin' with some boy at my house. You better send him home before you get all of us in trouble!"

Taking heed to Nalena's warning, I walked GioVanni to the front porch. "All right Miss Lady. I'ma call you when I get home. We gone definitely do this again." He promised with a soft kiss to my forehead as we said our goodbyes.

Summer break ended and it was time for us to return to school. GioVanni and I weren't able to see each other because we attended different schools and I went back on the east side with Aunt Icy. I offered cutting class as a solution, but he frowned upon it. He was a Mama's boy and didn't want to disappoint her. Over time, we slowly grew further apart. I didn't think anything of it when he hadn't called in a few weeks. Then DeNora blasted me with a rumor. "Girl! Did you hear about what happened to GioVanni?"

"Is it bad?" I whispered, afraid of what she could possibly have to tell me.

"He got shot and killed a couple of weeks ago. They already had his funeral and everything. I'm so sorry Cuz." She attempted to comfort me as I sat in silence for what seemed like hours, then picked up the phone and dialed GioVanni's number.

The recorded message repeated itself three times. "The number you have reached has been disconnected or is out of the service area. Please check the number and try again." I rationed that he'd gotten his number changed until being confronted by the obituary column in the Dayton Daily Newspaper. It confirmed the rumor to be true. GioVanni was dead!

As hard as I tried to hold them back, the tears came streaming with force. "Who the hell would want to kill GioVanni?" That salty taste of grief seemed all too familiar at that point. First Darius, now GioVanni.

DeNora heard that GioVanni went to a house party with a friend to sell drugs. After leaving, they were ambushed by a car full of guys and both GioVanni and his friend were shot dead. One thing I know is that GioVanni was a good guy with a curfew who loved and respected his mother too much to put himself in danger like that. I don't know why his life was taken so soon but I was beginning to realize the world was a dangerous place to live in. At 15 years old, I'd already lost two boyfriends to gun violence before they could reach the age of 18. That realization was the moment I decided to not give my heart to another person because it hurt too badly when they left.

GioVanni's angelic voice singing Karyn White's song, "I Rather Be Alone" was on repeat in my head for days as my heart ached from losing yet another person I deeply cared for. The bass in his voice penetrated my memory and made its way deep down into my soul, just like it did when he sang it to me that beautiful summer night...

"I won't be a fool, a fool for love, cause I know I rather be alone, than be here unhappy."

We never know when a friendship will dissipate, when a relationship will end or when a loved one will pass. Everyone and everything in life is temporary; therefore, I'm inclined to charge you with cherishing every moment, being fully present, taking nothing and no one for granted. Take risks, make beautiful mistakes, learn from them and share the lessons with others. People come and go but the love, experience and lessons we gain from joining forces with one another will be with us until the end of time. When love is lost it hurts but as Alfred Lord Tennyson said, *"Tis' better to have loved and lost than never to have loved at all"*.

"Be alert and of sober mind. Your enemy the devil prowls around like a roaring lion looking for someone to devour." 1 Peter 5:8 NIV

Art by Amani Ivy

"No Name"

Dayton, OH

Chapter 3: One Hell Of A Day

FOMO (fear of missing out) was eating me up while staying on the east side with Aunt Icy and not having a way to hang out with my friends on the west. I began to spend many nights at my cousin Yasmine's house. She's Nalena's younger sister who attended the same high school as I did. We had more freedom because her mom worked 2nd shift, and thought we were at Nalena's house most of the time. Rather, we were being what Grandma Jewel called, "some fast ass little girls," hanging out with Yasmine's boyfriend Siraj who lived in Nalena's neighborhood.

Siraj had a handsome host of brothers and friends for me to choose from like a kid at the pet store who had her pick at the liter. It was his loud, boisterous, bad boy brother Tyrone that I preyed on and got caught up in my intricate web of debauchery. Although he was in his 20's, he was unemployed and still lived at home with his mom, Siraj and the rest of their brothers. Tyrone was a slim, handsome chocolate man with his own car who smoked a lot of weed, drank a lot of alcohol and could do whatever he wanted to do, unlike GioVanni.

Our favorite pastime was driving around the city, drinking Hennessy and hot boxing while listening to Tupac's "Makaveli" CD on repeat with no particular destination in mind. Hot boxing includes smoking weed in an enclosed space so the smoke fills the interior area. I was attracted to the way in which Tyrone drove his car. His seat was pushed as far back as it could go. One of his hands were on the steering wheel and the other was hanging out of the window as he leaned towards the passenger side where I would sit. It must have been challenging for his foot to reach the gas and brake pedals being that he was a fairly short man that stood about 5'5", an inch taller than me.

Tyrone reminded me of my all time favorite rap artist, Tupac Shakur, therefore he was the coolest man I'd ever met. His carefree energy was magnetizing and he was always smiling and laughing. He loved the fact that I was a naughty high school girl but didn't pressure me to have sex. Tyrone didn't nag me about bettering myself in any way either. In fact, he encouraged me to forget about school and would pick me up practically everyday.

At least once or twice per week, I attended class in order to collect and turn in any homework assignments that were due. Surprisingly enough, the teachers were all familiar with the shenanigans and went along with this ordeal, no questions asked, until Mrs. Fairfax called me out on it one day. She was a laid back, unbothered, sweet English teacher who seemed to believe every lie I would tell in an attempt to skip out on assignments. At least that's how she portrayed herself to be until giving us the task of reading a novel and presenting the book report in front of the class.

On presentation day, I volunteered to go first and planned to later excuse myself from class with some elaborate story. A few trusted classmates knew that I was going to fabricate the report. They were confided in just in case it was a flop. Confidently, I walked to the front of the room, stood tall and gave an impromptu book report solely from the heights of my imagination.

"Do you see this class?" Mrs. Fairfax gently placed her hand on my shoulder. "This is what I expect from you all when you give your reports. Bridgett was knowledgeable about the subject, confident in her presentation and took us on a journey while summarizing the entire book."

The students began to wiggle around in their chairs, whispering and laughing amongst one another. "What's all this commotion about?" Mrs. Fairfax demanded.

"Man, she made that whole story up and you're telling us to be like her. We actually read a book like for real, for real!" One frustrated student blurted out.

Others that were clearly offended by my undeserved praise began to collectively confess that I'd told them prior to class that I was going to make it up. I'd become the adolescents' common enemy and they ganged up on me with a vengeance. Their actions communicated there wasn't a single friend in that classroom for me. My friends were the other stoners who were out skipping school at the moment, where I longed to be.

"Don't believe them Mrs. Fairfax, why would I do that when you're so well read? Surely you've read books by this world renowned author?" The deceit played on her intelligence, convincing her into agreeance.

"I know you didn't make that up, Bridgett. Don't worry about them. You just keep on reading and enjoying your books." Mrs. Fairfax comforted me with a squeeze to the shoulder, signaling me to go back to my seat. As I took the walk of shame with 52 eyeballs giving me the death stare, my beeper went off with a page from Tyrone. It was our code for, "Come outside."

Eager to leave the room, I raised my hand to gain Mrs. Fairfax's attention. "Yes Miss Hatch?" She answered using my assigned surname which made my soul cringe ever since researching where they originated. Research revealed that in the days of slavery, "masters" gave the slaves their surname as a means to identify their property, but I digress.

"May I go to the bathroom?" I stuttered, longing to escape the wrath of the pubescent teenagers.

"Yes, you may after you complete your daily journal writing and turn it in to me before you go." She answered sternly, knowing very well that she wouldn't see me again until the next week.

"Today's journaling assignment is to describe your ideal fantasy bedroom. Bridgett I'll have you do yours now and everyone else will do so after the presentations." Mrs. Fairfax announced as the classroom hissed and squealed at their disdain towards me.

As the next student presented his book report, I put my head down with a level of moral culpability and began to journal my imaginary bedroom as quickly as possible. It noted:

Dear Diary,

My ideal fantasy bedroom spins on an axis within the confinement of our house. The walls are pure white with purple, green and gold luxurious fixtures throughout the room. A huge tree stump protrudes from the ceiling, hanging there like a ceiling fan with rose stems for blades. As the stems oscillate, roses bloom and petals are released from each blade, one petal at a time. The air is soft, cool and moist with a mist of rain like a quiet afternoon in the Springtime. My bed is made of flowers and pillows consisting of pillars of clouds floating about with a waterfall headboard providing the beautiful sound of peace and serenity in my living space. The floor of bright green and healthy grass blades cushion my feet and provides a sweet aroma of fresh cut grass coupled with

I waited until the student was done with his report then eagerly handed in my rapid expression of immature writing. Surprisingly, Mrs. Fairfax read my journal in front of the entire class as I stood at her desk with a sheepish smile tugging at my lips. The class burst out laughing in unison when she finished. "Bridgett, why don't you just stay in class and apply yourself? You're a very creative girl with so much potential!" Mrs. Fairfax informed me.

Never had anyone spoke so eloquently of me before. I couldn't remember being told that I was good at anything in life besides stealing, having a fiery mouth and talking too much at that point. The appreciation was overwhelming, and tears began to formulate. Frustration ensued regarding the unfamiliar feelings, leaving me with a desire to do something reckless to dissipate the warm and mushy emotions. With my classmates laughing with derision, I didn't know how to receive her compliment and resolved to dismiss it altogether. "Can I go to the bathroom now?"

With a disheartened look on her face, Mrs. Fairfax granted my request, allowing me to escape from ridicule. Mrs. Fairfax's belief in me still skips a beat within my heart to this very day. That goes to show, we never know how our words of encouragement will influence someone's life. I still ponder, whether or not she knew that I'd made that book report up and just went along with it to encourage my creative process.

Subsequently, the daily journal writing opened up an unknown portal. A world where I was free to express myself. Free to be vulnerable. Free to dream without limits. My diary was like a purse. It was with me at all times and I began to document each adventure of the day. Who I was with, what we did, who said what and all the unadulterated, raw and messy foolishness of the day. Each entry frequently started off with: *Dear Diary, I had one hell of a day today.*

Yasmine and I stopped by Nalena's house on our way to see Siraj and Tyrone one day. After leaving, the careless mistake dawned on me while walking down the street. "I forgot my damn diary at Nalena's house!" We shared a look of terror and took off running back to hunt for the incriminating evidence.

We ransacked the downstairs kitchen, couch cushions and underneath the furniture to no avail. Yasmine ran to search upstairs and immediately shrieked, "Bridgett, Nalena's reading your diary!" Power hopping up the stairs, taking three steps at a time, I was greeted with the sight of Nalena sitting on the toilet with the bathroom door wide open. My journal was palmed in one hand and the telephone in the other.

"Give me my diary!" I attempted to snatch it out of her hand but she pulled back too quickly.

"Y'all fast ass little girls be into some shit huh? Y'all just be leaving me out!" She joked at our expense.

Yasmine shot me to meanest look I'd ever seen her conjure up. "You wrote about me in there?" She whispered.

"Uh, that's personal, Nalena! Give it back!" Deflecting seemed to be the right thing to do while reaching to snatch it out of her hand again.

"I already read it to your mama and Aunt Icy. They are on the phone right now!" She bragged.

"Finish reading it Nalena." Mama requested over the speaker.

"Ok Auntie Donnie, I'll start from the top of yesterday's entry!" She deliberately warned and began to read as Yasmine and I stood idly by, mean mugging her from the hallway.

Dear Diary,

I had one hell of a day today! Tyrone and Siraj picked me and Yasmine up so we could bail out from school again. We drove around smoking blunt after blunt, hot boxing through the city. I kept having to wipe the condensation off the inside of the windshield with my uniform sweater so we could see out of the window. When we pulled up to Tyrone's house and opened the doors, a thick ass cloud of weed smoke escaped from all four sides, polluting the cool afternoon air.

We laid on top of the hood and windshield of his station wagon, listening to Tupac's "Makaveli" cassette tape. I was so damn high I started seeing shit in the sky. The first thing I saw was a big ass turtle. The shell, the head, the legs were all connected and it was moving too. I thought I was tripping so I pointed it out in the sky to see if anyone else could see it and they did! The next thing I saw was a humungous ice cream cone with two scoops of ice cream. We laughed at how high all of us must have been to be able to decipher random objects in the clouds as they slowly passed by. Yasmine and Siraj grew bored of our cloudy antics and ducked off into the house to get their freak on like they always do...

"Oh my God Bridgett why would you write about me in your diary?" Yasmine screeched as I successfully grabbed the diary out of Nalena's hand while she laughed at our despair.

"My bad girl. Who would have thought anyone would ever read my personal diary!" I rationed while frantically ripping the pages to pieces.

"Well, they did and now I'm going to get in big trouble!" She cried. I'm not sure how badly she was punished but I wasn't allowed to spend the night at Yasmine's house for a long while. Upon reuniting, we made up our own language using different symbols as an alternative to the alphabet in order to write about our hell of a day with discretion.

Tyrone and I eventually broke up after finding out he had another girlfriend. She pulled up on us while we were outside of his house lying on his car. "You still messing with this little bitch?" She punched him in the face and then looked at me. "What you gone do about it?" She threatened.

The girl was quite stalky, rough around the edges and talked like she had nothing to lose. Apparently, she was more invested in him than I was. Tyrone was not about to get the satisfaction of having two girls fight over him that day, plus she looked like she would win. I gracefully backed down and surrendered him to her. "That's y'all business!"

Nothing good was associated with that relationship anyhow. You know how God will speak to us in unconventional ways and at times we don't listen? He often stirs up a situation to make us listen right? Yeah, I believe that's what God used that girl for, to punk me out and make me listen! "Leave that man alone!"

Yasmine, on the other hand, kept dating Siraj and ended up having a baby with him. When her baby was still a toddler, allegedly, Siraj found himself playing a game of Russian Roulette. It's a lethal game of chance in which a player places a single bullet in a revolver, spins the cylinder, places the muzzle against their head and pulls the trigger. Unfortunately, when he allegedly pulled the trigger, he shot himself in the head. Miraculously enough, Siraj survived only to live with mental and physical incapabilities, nonetheless, he lived.

Have you ever made a poor decision that could have cost your life but you still lived to tell the story? If so, I believe that may be the very reason you are still living, to tell the story! It may not be as extreme as playing Russian Roulette but whatever your story may be, someone's life could be saved because of your boldness to share.

As I look back on this disheartening occurrence, I can see how it's parallel to the way in which urban children's lives are gambled with everyday. We gamble with going outside and not being a victim of police brutality, a robbery, murder or whether we're going to be properly educated by the public school system or not. We gamble with ourselves by running the streets at night, selling drugs, using drugs, abusing alcohol and exhibiting promiscuous behavior.

We even gamble with the people we trust with our children. Sometimes the very adults who are presumed to protect us are the same ones who abuse us physically, verbally, emotionally or even sexually. I remember when an adult I trusted misused his knowledge, authority and resources to manipulate me.

Since Yasmine had a child and couldn't kick it as much, I started hanging out with a friend from school. She didn't smoke or drink and was still super cool. She always had money and loved boys even more than I did. One day we were at her house waiting on some boys to meet us there. While watching television in the living room, we heard the front door creek open. "Oh shit, it's my stepdad!" She announced as this big, tall, overshadowing figure walked into the house.

"What are you two doing here during school hours?" He demanded.

"We were on lunch break and I just came to change my clothes." She lied.

"Don't you lie to me girl!" He snapped back.

"Ok, we got bored and left school early." She confessed.

Her stepdad ordered her into the kitchen and away from my presence. The kitchen wasn't that far away but their voices were inaudible. I remember thinking,

"Wow he must really be saying some pretty harsh things to her that he has to whisper so I don't hear it."

I was tempted to sneak out of the front door to avoid the same harsh punishment she seemed to be getting. He already knew me so that would prove to be senseless. He'd just show up at my house and tell Mama that he caught us skipping school and I'd have to suffer the consequences anyhow.

My friend slowly walked out of the kitchen with a troublesome look on her face. "What happened Bitch?" I whispered.

"He wants to see you in the kitchen." She responded with no further explanation while facing the floor.

"What does he want? What did he say to you? Are we in trouble?"

"Go see!" She said with a quiet somber expression, avoiding eye contact with me.

Slowly tiptoeing to the kitchen, I looked back at my friend with every step. The hope of her giving me an indication that everything would be okay was lost. Instead of looking back at me, she walked straight to her room, disappearing from sight.

Her stepdad was leaning against the marble countertop with a sly look on his face. "Hey, you want some money?" He inquired, much to my astonishment. We were expecting punishment but were actually going to be rewarded! What a great turn of events, I thought and lit up with excitement at the sight of money.

"Yes please, I'd love to have some money!" My hand was open to receive the $40 hanging out of his open wallet.

"Let me see your boobs!" He quietly propositioned me.

"What?" I answered, totally shocked and appalled.

"Just let me see your boobs and I'll give you the money. No one will ever know and I won't tell that you were over here skipping school." He promised.

"Ewww, no I'm not doing that. You're my friend's stepdad. What do I look like?" I concluded and began to walk away.

"Come on, she just showed me hers. She does it all the time. Where do you think she gets her money from?" He argued. "Ok, ok, I'll give you $100 if you just show me one boob!" He begged.

"Did she really do it?" I asked, intrigued by the crispy hundred-dollar bill dangling in my face.

"Yes, we do this all the time!" He reassured me.

"Ok but just this one time." I said with the same somber expression I'd witnessed my friend walk out of the kitchen with moments before.

That one time ended up being plenty and it got a little more raunchier over time. Seducing my friend's stepdad became my primary source of income for a while. She and I didn't discuss the situation until we were well into adulthood, after many bouts of therapy on my part. I'm still not sure if she knew what took place in the kitchen that day or if he'd just manipulated me into believing she was a known and willing participant.

If only the adults could have read my diary at that time. Maybe someone would have put a stop to him. Maybe they would have told me how valuable I was. How my body is the Lord's temple and that I should respect it. Maybe someone would have sat me down to discuss the source of my low self-esteem, greed and desperate need to seek and gain the attention of boys...and grown men for that matter.

Cognitive distortion coupled with threats from the abuser can keep a person silent when violated. They may feel as if they'll be the one punished or even worse if the situation is brought to light. These inaccurate thoughts reinforce negative thinking, insecurities and risky behavior. This is why it's imperative to create a safe space for uncomfortable conversations with those we love. That would include but not be limited to sharing personal stories, being relatable and asking probing and direct questions regarding abuse. In the event that anything happens to someone you love, they'll know they have a confidant in you because you're not afraid to sit with them in uncomfortable places.

Eventually I got my first job and started making my own money once I turned 15 and a half which was the legal age to begin work in Ohio. With no interviewing skills, I initially did not get the job at McDonalds. Apparently, the manager said I was too loud and ghetto according to my friend who worked there. She was able to convince the manager to hire me as a favor, in spite of my unprofessionalism.

A few months later, I skipped school to pick up my paycheck and purchase some party favors for the weekend. Upon arriving, the manager presented me with alarming news. The paychecks were printed but she had to wait until a specific time to distribute them out.

"Oh really? So you mean to tell me you got my money but not gone give it to me until you're good and got damn ready?" I snapped at the manager who reluctantly hired me in the first place.

"It's the policy and procedure Bridgett. If I do it for you then I'll have to do it for everyone." She replied.

"Well I guess it's everybody's lucky day today because I'm not coming back in no five or six hours. You go give me my money right now Ma'am!"

"Ok, now I'm going to have to ask you to leave." She quietly suggested while keeping her composure.

"If I leave here without my check then you can just put it in the mail and take me off the schedule because I quit!"

"Bye Bridgett." She mouthed under clenched teeth.

"Say no more!" Stomping my way to the door, I made an announcement before leaving, "Don't eat McDonalds poisonous food people! They trying to kill us!" Says a person that ate it every day. That moment would prove to be the first of over 100 jobs that I would either quit or get fired from in the first 33 years of my life. Although it sounds psychotic and is not recommended, jumping from job to job allotted me the luxury of experiencing a wide variety of people, environments and skill sets that are extremely valuable.

Since being unemployed, my spare time was dedicated to numbing out and partying. The goal for my 16th birthday was to smoke 16 blunts, go clubbing and get wasted off Hennessy and Coke. That dream came to a screeching halt when I drank Mama's wine cooler. It knocked me out well before sunset on August 8, 1998. A few days later, a fellow Leo friend asked if I wanted to hang out on her birthday and celebrate together. I was all in being that I slept my entire sweet 16th away!

We spent her birthday doing what we did on most days, drinking and smoking. The day ended with me sleeping over at her house for the first time. She lived with her mother and two older brothers whom I hadn't met before. We arrived around 1:00am, staggering through her dark, chilly and quiet home. The only audible sound was from the smoke detector testing itself throughout the night's air.

My Leo friend announced that I would be sleeping on the couch as she stumbled upstairs to her warm and cozy bed. I noticed that she neglected to give me a blanket, pillow or pajamas to sleep in for that matter. Too intoxicated to care, I shrugged my shoulders and sunk into the brown leather sofa as it stuck to my skin, cradling me like a swaddled infant.

Awakened from a deep REM sleep, moaning with pleasure, I felt a familiar sensation running throughout my body. At first it seemed to be what many people called a wet dream. I rubbed the crust out of my eyes and slowly opened them. An unfamiliar dark male figure was hovering over my body, making moaning sounds as well. Looking into his eyes and realizing what the strange person was doing, "No, stop, don't," I fearfully whispered while making an effort to pull his hand out of my pants.

"Shhhhhh." He warned. "You know you like it!" Gasping for enough air to fill my lungs up and scream, the sound was muffled by a stump being placed over my mouth. My eyes grew big with astonishment as I began to kick and wiggle around until he finally unleashed me from his possession. I was even more freaked out to see that the man was missing a hand.

With his stump still over my mouth, he whispered, "I bet my sister is a damn tease just like you!" Sister, I thought, this can't be my friend's brother who just violated me!

"Don't even think of telling anybody about this because they won't believe a fast ass little girl like you. I'm going to uncover your mouth but you better not scream! Do you understand?" He threatened with a look of desperation. I shook my head in agreement.

Being told I was a fast ass little girl was nothing new. The man's words rang true and I believed him. He removed his stump from my mouth, retrieved a blanket from the closet, placed it over me then walked up the stairs into the darkness. I sat there silenced in shame, embarrassment and guilt, feeling even more alone than when I was manipulated at nine years old. That encounter became yet another secret I kept well into adulthood.

If I could say anything to the 16-year-old precious jewel sitting on that brown leather couch and anyone else who has felt the pain of shame, I'd tell them that everything will be okay. You are not alone. God is always with you and He allows you to go through these rough patches because He's already equipped you with what you need to overcome them. He allowed the mess so it could become your message to the world. You may be silent now, but the powerful roar inside of you will not be silenced forever.

If you can relate, know that your pain is not in vain. Find someone you trust or hire a therapist and share your story. Speak up because when you do, you empower yourself and others. You especially give the people that are suffering in silence, the advantage of knowing they too are not alone. There's healing in allowing your voice to be heard. You are valuable! You are more than enough!

Someone's opinion of you does not determine the course of your life. It only takes precedence if you believe it. It doesn't matter if a family member, friend or authority figure has said anything unkind about you. Do not let it resonate within. The most important opinion you have is the opinion you have about yourself. Think highly of yourself and your actions will follow. When you think poorly of yourself like I did, predators can smell your weak and insecure scent from a mile away, even in your sleep.

Child abuse and neglect is a very serious matter that can make people squeamish and uncomfortable, yet it has to be swept from up under the rug at some point in time. I understand that it is challenging to see the light at the end of the tunnel when most days are one hell of a day. There's power in praying, trusting and believing that it does get better. If you're going through turbulence in your life, I'd advise you to take a note from Winston Churchill who said, *"If you're going through hell, keep going."* Don't pitch a tent there!

"Praise be to the God and Father of our Lord Jesus Christ, the Father of compassion and the God of all comfort, who comforts us in all our troubles, so that we can comfort those in any trouble with the comfort we ourselves receive from God." 2 Corinthians 1:3-4 NIV

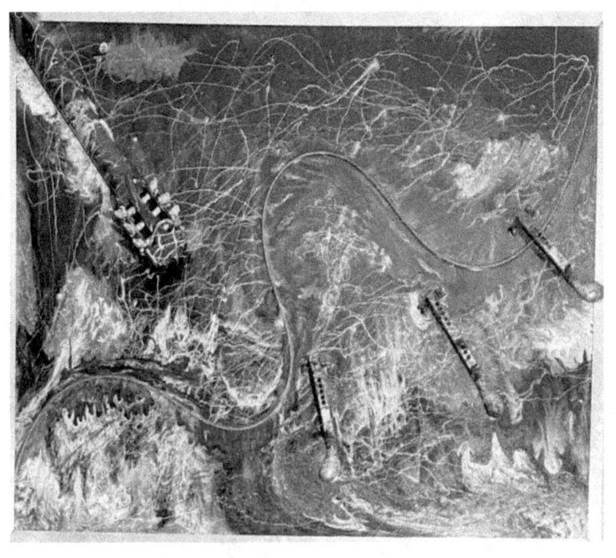

Mike Angel Reynoso Perspective Art

"The Sound of Color"

Los Angeles, CA

Chapter 4: The Fast Lane

DeNora was riding shotgun with a boy from the east side projects at 90mph on the 35 West interstate around 3am. I was in the backseat smoking a blunt and bobbing my head to Master P's hit song, "Make Em' say Uhh" that was blasting through the stereo system as loud as it could go. Enjoying the fast lane, the three of us were rapping along when my favorite part by Mystical came on, *"I won't stop now bitch, I can't stop and you can't stop em so bitch don't try. We true soldiers, we don't die, we keep rollin, na na na na na."*

The east side boy was feeling cool, crouched down low in the driver's seat which apparently impaired him from seeing the flashing red and blue lights in the rear-view mirror. Our party was interrupted by a speeding police cruiser that pulled up to the passenger side where DeNora and I were. "Get off at the next exit!" The Dayton Police Officer demanded using his megaphone.

"Shit, man!   I can't go back to jail!"   The neighborhood boy confessed as he smashed his foot onto the accelerator taking the car up to 100mph. With the police cruiser in tow, dude sped down the highway with no regard for his life or ours.

"Oh my God!   Stop! Let us out! Pull over!" DeNora and I loudly pleaded in unison.

"This is your last warning, get off on the next exit or we will use force!" The cops warned for the last time.

"Bitch we bout to die!" I helplessly cried out to DeNora in defeat, reached forward to hug her by the neck and squeezed tightly. "I love you Cousin!"

"I love you too Cousin!" She was clawing into my arms with her nails.

"Man y'all some punk ass bitches", the east side dude smacked his lips, disgusted at the site of our terror. He then turned the music off, slowed the car down and pulled over onto the shoulder of the freeway. The police cruiser stopped a few yards behind us.

"Driver, step out of the vehicle with your hands up!" The officer ordered via his megaphone.

The east side boy looked at us and threatened, "Y'all better not tell em' my name either!"

"Boy don't nobody even know your real name!" I snapped back as he slowly lifted his hands in the air and stepped out of the car. Looking through the rear-view mirror so as to not make any sudden moves, DeNora and I could see that one of the Dayton Police Officers had his gun drawn out and pointed at the boy. The other officer handcuffed and placed him in the cruiser.

The officer holding the gun approached us. "Either of you girls got a drivers license?" He casually asked as if he wasn't waving a deadly weapon at our temples.

"No, we're just teenagers but we have our identification." DeNora informed him.

"Stay put." He ordered as he snatched our ID's from her hand and walked back to his police cruiser. When he returned, he informed us that we were free to go.

The east side boy was still in the back seat of the cruiser, so we didn't understand what he meant by we are free to go. "Y'all letting him go too?" I gullibly asked with hope.

"Nope. He has a warrant for his arrest and he's driving without a license. He's going to jail tonight. Better call someone to come and get you two."

"We don't have a phone. Do you have one we could use?" DeNora negotiated.

"Nope. We're about to have this car towed." The officer ordered us to get out of the car and out of his way.

"Can you at least contact our Auntie, she's a police sergeant?" I announced thinking that would give us some type of saving grace.

"Nope, we don't have a phone to use." He answered using what seemed to be his favorite word.

"Can y'all give us a ride to my brothers house? He doesn't live too far from here." DeNora begged.

"Nope. Better be careful with who you jump in the car with next time." He tipped us, blushing with a gleam of pleasure.

Out of fear and frustration, I yelled, "Sir it's three o'clock in the damn morning. How do you expect us to get home?"

"Frankly my dear, I don't give a fuck!" The Dayton Police officer shot back with unkind eyes and a glare that promised he meant what he said.

"Cuz, I'm scared as hell!" DeNora confessed as we were walking down the shoulder of the long stretch of highway holding hands.

"Me too Bitch! Let's just walk like we're hard so nobody knows we're girls!" I cleverly suggested. We could feel the flutter of the pavement at the soles of our feet as the semi-trucks and cars aggressively zoomed by. Their headlights shined upon us revealing our shivering, frail demeanors and tightly wound fists.

We made our way off the highway without incident and into a residential area heading to DeNora's brother's house. Just as we thought we were hidden by the pitch-black darkness of the night, a car pulled up beside us with a black male occupying all four sides. "What y'all girls doing walking around this late at night?" The front passenger gently questioned.

Taught by society to fear our own black men at an early age, DeNora and I ignored them and walked at a faster pace. "Do y'all need a ride or something?" He continued to press the issue as the car slowly cruised beside us.

Still holding my hand and digging her nails into my palm, DeNora attempted to scare the guys off by cursing them out. "Hell nah we don't need no ride from some strange ass men that we don't know. My brother is coming to get us right now so get the hell away from us!"

"Man forget them then. We trying to help y'all out!" The driver chimed in and began to drive away.

"Bye! We don't need your help anyway. My cousin is on his way"! I confirmed DeNora's lie.

"Aye man, that sounds like my little cousins out there!" A familiar voice interrupted from the back passenger side of the car. DeNora and I looked at the speaker and were more than relieved to see that it was our cousin, Eric! As small as Dayton, OH is, we do have a large extended family. The odds that one of the four men were related to us was still shocking. I know now, that it was God that sent an Angel in literally one of our darkest hours. He always looks out for His children like that, even when we don't recognize it and call it a coincidence.

"Eric!" DeNora and I both cried with joy.

"Aye man, this my family Bruh." Eric announced to the driver as he opened the back door to let us in. "What the hell y'all doing out here like this in the middle of the night?" As they drove us to our destination, we shared the unbelievable story of the east side boy and the Dayton Police Officers who could care less about the wellbeing of two teenage black girls from the hood.

It's interesting how even with a gun to our heads, we yielded to the white cops seeking guidance and mercy. When four black men offered to help out of love and concern, we made them out to be the bad guys. Our perception was inadvertently misconstrued. We were programmed with the same miseducation that was passed down from generations of enslavement; white meant good, black meant bad. I learned that self-awareness is the first step towards positive change.

The officer's delivery may have been harsh, but his message was right on point. We definitely should have been more careful about who we hopped into the car with. Our mistake could have been the death of us. I swore that I would never place myself in that type of predicament again. That proved to be one of many broken promises made to myself and others.

A short time later, a female classmate and I decided we'd skip school to smoke some weed together. Just as we exited the building, a car full of fine young men stopped to talk to us. I recognized the guy in the front passenger seat. He was an upperclassman that attended Patterson High School with us. The other boys were unfamiliar.

"We're about to go to my partner's house to chill and smoke, y'all down?" The handsome familiar face enticed. He was very popular at school and I was stoked at the opportunity of hanging out with him. It was possible to transform my reputation from being the black hippie with purple hair to a popular, cool kid with purple hair.

The female classmate and I quickly hopped on the chance to hang out with the cool kids. We smoked and hot boxed in the car on the way to our destination. Once we got there, we smoked more weed and added alcohol to the equation while listening to a mixed hip-hop cassette tape.

The handsome upperclassman invited the other girl upstairs with him. She accepted his offer. "Damn!" I thought. "Now I don't even want to be here." Left downstairs with the other three boys, I purposely sat on a rocking chair in the living room to discourage them from touching me. My body felt as if it were being swallowed up by the chair as the blaring music throbbed inside of my brain.

Suddenly suspicious of everything and everyone around me, I contemplated the situation at hand. "Did the girl set me up to get gang raped? Did they drug me? Am I going to ever make it out of…" Right in the middle of my apprehensive and paranoid thought pattern, one of the guys tapped me on the shoulder from behind the chair. It felt as if my soul had jumped out of my skin and a high pitched squeal was released, "Ahhhhhhhhhhhhhh". The boys laughed hysterically like they were expecting me to react in that manner.

At that point, I suspected we were smoking more than marijuana inside of those blunts. I'd smoked a lot of weed and drank a lot of alcohol but never experienced that level of heightened sensitivity to sound, light and touch. I desperately wanted to get out of there.

Juvenile's hit song, "Back That Ass Up," started playing and the boys got super hype. "Why don't you get up and back that ass up for us Ms. Lady?" One of the boys suggested using his smooth, sexy and seductive voice.

"Nah I'm good. I really need to get back to the school to take a test though." I fibbed through shocked nerves.

"Well I tell you what…tell the homie we will be right back if he comes downstairs." He instructed as the three of them left out of the front door together. I got up to turn the music off then went to the foreign kitchen and made myself a glass of ice water, hoping to drown out my high trip. I sat quietly staring at the ceiling until the two classmates finally came downstairs.

"Y'all ready?" Dude announced.

"Yeah I been ready but your friends said they'd be right back."

"Nah they outside already." He assured me. The girl was quiet with a blank expression on her face.

"You alright?" I inquired.

"Yeah I'm good girl." She whispered.

"Come on y'all, we got to go before my partner's mom comes home!" Dude practically pushed us out of the house.

When we got to his friend's car, it was jam packed with even more of their homeboys. "I had to pick my boys up. We only got room for one more person." The driver declared.

"Welp, I guess that's me!" The upperclassman said as he hopped in the front passenger seat.

"What the hell? Are you kidding me? How in the hell are we supposed to get home? You brought us here so you have to take us back." I disputed.

"I'm sure y'all can figure it out between the two of you." The driver was laughing hysterically and sped off, leaving us standing on the sidewalk coughing up the smoke from his exhaust pipe.

Deja vu struck as we were walking to safety after hopping in the car with the wrong people, yet again. The upperclassman shared with everyone at school the next day, how they made us walk home. The girl never briefed me on what happened upstairs, but she did decide to not hang out with me anymore. That may have been a good decision being that I later found myself in a similar scenario.

Going through life is a lot like driving a car. You are the vehicle and life is the journey. Pastor Rush of IBOC Church in Dallas, TX spoke on this subject in his sermon entitled, "I Gotta Believe It." I mentioned this in Part I of this book series in the introduction. He painted a metaphorical picture of life in the fast lane. Pastor Rush said in essence, "You start off driving on the freeway for 35-45 minute in the fast lane at 80mph. You see that your exit is five miles down the road. You begin to signal so you can move over and change lanes. The other drivers allow you to merge over and you make your way to the service lane. You drive in the service lane for the rest of the journey until you get off at your destination."

Pastor Rush metaphor represented how some of us start off living a fast life until we get somewhere around 35-45 years old, hopefully sooner. We live that fast life until God gives us a signal that it's time to change. He signals us with a life-or-death situation, an illness, spiritual revelation, death in the family, hitting rock bottom or whatever prompts you to change. Once prompted, your actions notify others that you are switching lanes, moving from the place you once were to where you are now going. Some people may help and support you as you transition, others may not.

You then make your way to the service lane of life. That doesn't mean that you are at the end of your journey, it means you don't have to travel as fast as you used to. This is where you find your calling, your life's purpose. Now you are at a place where you finally understand why you are traveling on this journey called life in the first place. This is where you slow down and move with intention, grace and a quiet confidence knowing that you are in the right lane in preparation for your exit. This is where you serve others with your God given gifts and talents.

If you're in the fast lane of your life where everything's a blur, know that you can merge at any time. Switch lanes. You don't have to wait for some miraculous sign, a certain age or for anyone's permission. You can decide at any moment to slow down and move with purpose and intention while adding value to others and enjoying the scenery of your journey. Either way, your struggles are there to shape your future. In the words of Paulo Coelho, *"Straight roads do not make skillful drivers."*

"But if you do not drive out the inhabitants of the land, those you allow to remain will become barbs in your eyes and thorns in your sides. They will give you trouble in the land where you will live." Numbers 33:55 NIV

Roland Hatch Photography

"Down Salem Way"

Dayton, OH

Chapter 5: Blood On Their Hands

Is it safe to say that every family has their own unique mess and way of showing love? Where I'm from, our love was proven by a willingness to shed blood for one another. Mama's parents got married at a young age. Papaw never grew out of the ladies man stage although he frequently got caught cheating. His game was unmatched by Grandma Jewel's keen investigative abilities.

Mama has a memory of when she was 13 years old. Grandma Jewel took her on a quest to find her daddy and his latest home wrecker. They located him and the woman outside of the Westown Shopping Center, holding hands. Enraged at the sight of her man with another woman, Grandma Jewel handed Mama a gun and ordered her to shoot her daddy. Mama being the obedient child she was taught to be, opened fire without hesitation. Thank God she had poor aim. No one got hurt.

As tumultuous as my grandparents' relationship was, they stayed together through it all. Until death did they part. This was the display of love that Mama was exposed to in her early years. It was no surprise that she equated drama with love and attracted dramatic men like Keith into her life many years later.

"Donella it's 11 o'clock at night, where's Bridgett?" Keith inquired.

"Hell if I know. She better be across the street over ole girls house or that's her ass." The ole girl was my friend Genevieve who lived across the street with her grandma and three handsome brothers. She and I attended Patterson and would hang out in the neighborhood after school.

Mama walked across the street to Genevieve's house only to learn that they were looking for her as well. "She's not there and neither is her friend. Ain't no telling where they're at but I'll handle Bridgett when she gets home!" Mama schooled Keith.

He grew frighteningly suspicious of her calm demeanor.

"Come on Donella, you know where she is. You killed her didn't you?"

"Killed her? Who in the hell thinks like that? You gotta be out of your damn mind!" The two of them went back and forth with one another until I walked through the front door.

"Where the hell have you been all night?" Mama scolded as soon I walked in.

I glanced over at the clock on the wall. "What? It's only midnight. I was with Genevive at the park playing kickball with some other kids."

"Take your ass in your room and don't come out until I tell you to!" She pointed at Keith, "Got this man thinking I done killed you and shit!"

Honestly, I didn't understand what all the drama was about. I was 16 years old and damn near grown. At least that's what I used to tell everyone. Being punished due to Keith's sinister imagination was unsettling. I vowed to teach him a thing or two about how things were run in our household.

Who was I kidding? It wasn't even our household and I had to learn to live by Keith's rules now. He'd actually kept his promise and rented a three-bedroom ranch style house for Mama and her three kids to live with him on the west side of Dayton. It was apparent that I couldn't go unaccounted for now that we lived with a man that watched our every move.

Keith was extremely overprotective of everyone in the household, especially Mama. We went to the corner store with him one day, Mama and I were in the checkout line when she noticed the man in front of us was a high school classmate. They quickly reminisced about the good ole days before he purchased his belongings. Keith joined us in line with a pack of freshly chopped meat in his hand from the butcher. Mama's old classmate turned to kindly say his goodbyes before leaving the store, "Nice to see you again Donella. You take care." Keith's eyes bulged out and Mama knew he was about to perform an award-winning movie scene.

Keith was about 6'4", with a large muscular build and deep authoritative tone of voice. When he spoke, his voice ricochet throughout the entire store, "Take care? Nice to see you again? When the hell have you been seeing my woman, Sucka? He waited for a response but didn't get any. "You damn right she gone take care. I'ma be the one taking care of her, Partner. Unless you want to do something about that." The classmate remained quiet as the cashier bagged his groceries. Keith continued, "Don't worry about her care. You keep talking to my woman like that and you'll be packaged up like this meat in my hand then your body parts will be mailed to your family, piece by piece, Playa!"

Mama's old classmate quietly walked out of the store leaving Keith to appear as if he was talking to himself. That may have been the best decision of his life. All eyes were on the three of us as Mama attempted to calm Keith down by stroking his huge ego and shoulder. "Baby you know I only have eyes for you."

Keith smiled, apparently enticed by the confirmation. "You damn right!"

He looked around the store, feeding off the attention, "No man better not dare to even say hello to my woman when I'm around. If you got something to say to her then you say it to me!" He theatrically announced as the three of us left the store without any further incident. Keith walked out feeling victorious with Mama coo-ing his temper and hanging onto his arm. I lingered behind with my head hung low, pretending to be invisible by covering my face.

Despite his hot temper and raging jealous tendencies, Keith gave the impression of a protective family man that took pride in his ability to provide and protect. In an attempt to show his softer side, he came home with a cute little puppy one day. It was a six-month-old all black Labrador Retriever whom we named Bear. He was such a playful pup that loved to fetch and play tug of war all day long.

Having Bear lit our house up with pure happiness. He was my one and only source of daily hugs and affection. I didn't realize it then, but he was the perfect emotional support animal. The love I had for Bear started to pour over in the appreciation I had for Keith. I was beginning to think he wasn't that bad of a man after all until he proved me, not wrong, but dead wrong.

One day, Genevieve and I walked home together from the school bus stop laughing and making plans to go to the park after completing our homework. I walked into the house just as happy as can be, excited for Bear to meet me at the front door wagging his little tail as he did every day! "Where's my good boy?" I searched the floor expecting Bear to run and jump into my arms as usual.

"You never bite the hand that feeds you!" Keith screamed. My eyes followed a trail of blood on the floor that led to Keith. He stood in the center of the living room holding his palms out. Blood was dripping from each palm, to and through every finger and onto the tan carpet. Keith's white t-shirt was a freshly stained crimson red. The blood splatter on his face, arms and all over his body told a gruesome story that I was not prepared to receive.

"You never bite the hand that feeds you!" He repeatedly screamed with a blank stare and black eyes so dark I could see the demons struggling to escape from his soul.

"What happened?" I reluctantly screeched, fearing that he'd murdered Mama as a result of a jealous rage.

"That nigga back there dead!" He stated in a militant tone as if he was reporting for duty.

"Oh my God. Who's dead? Reggie?" A solitary tear escaped as I searched the windows of his soul for a glimmer of humanity. My brother Reggie was known to talk back and challenge Mama's boyfriend's. I immediately assumed that was the case and concluded that Reggie had messed with the wrong boyfriend this time.

"What nigga?" I continued to inquire through whispering cries while backing up towards the front door for safety.

"Bear! That nigga in the back yard dead. Bet his punk ass don't bite another mother fucker that feeds him anymore!" He promised.

I swiftly removed the backpack off my shoulders, dropped it onto the soiled carpet and bolted past the bloody, murderous shell of a human and ran out of the back door. Bear's lifeless body was lying by the opening of the fence as if he were trying to escape the devil's wrath. Six bloody bricks were accompanied by our family pet's corpse. Keith apparently threw bricks at him until he didn't have any more breath in his body. "Aaaaaaahhhhhhhhh", the strange squeal bubbled up from the pit of my belly and expelled out of my mouth.

I sprinted to Genevieve's house and pounded on the door, sulking and drowning in tears. Her oldest brother answered, the one whom I had a huge crush on. "What happened?" He scanned.

"Keith killed Bear and it's blood everywhere!" I cried as he pulled me close to his chest for a warm and protective embrace. For a quick second, I melted into his arms and forgot the reason I was there in the first place.

Genevieve heard the commotion and ran from out of her bedroom. "Oh my God! We have to call the police!"

Her brother pried me off his chest and grabbed the phone to dial 911. "911 what's your emergency?" The operator answered on the first ring. You must have to pay someone to get that type of service in Los Angeles, where I currently reside. You're lucky if you even get through to 911 at all.

"Hi, um my mama's boyfriend killed our dog." I reported. The operator informed me to not go back in the house and that a cruiser was on its way.

I called Mama to fill her in on what her man had been up to. "Mama, Keith killed Bear and it's a bloody mess at home. I'm over Genevieve's house."

"What the hell? Stay there. I'm on my way!" Mama promised.

Once Mama and the policemen arrived, I returned home so I could witness Keith get arrested for murder. Still fashioned in the incriminating t-shirt with a bloody face and hands, he stepped outside as I was informing the officer of my version of events. Keith chimed in and swore Bear attacked him and it was self-defense. The police ran a background check then explained they were taking him into custody. Surprisingly, Keith did not put up a fight as they slapped the metal cuffs on his wrist and placed him in the backseat of the cruiser.

"Ma'am your boyfriend's on parole so we're going to have to take him in for the night." One of the officers briefed Mama.

She was genuinely aghast, "Parole? He's on parole for what?"

The officer searched the database to get his facts straight before answering. "Well, it looks like he did a stint back in Alabama for murder and was recently released from prison." Mama's face grew unsettled and I could tell she was bewildered.

Keith was released the following day on his own recognizance. He returned back home after successfully convincing Mama to forgive him for omitting the truth. He was later found not guilty for the murder of Bear. Still traumatized, I sentenced myself to my bedroom, curled up under the blanket and turned the tv up loud enough to drown out Keith's voice and my thoughts. Poor Bear's body was still lying in the backyard, covered in a pool of blood. Keith ordered Reggie to help him stuff the bloody bricks and corpse into a black, 13-liter Hefty trash bag.

Watching from my bedroom window as they loaded the bag into the backseat of Keith's car, I silently cried alone as they drove away. Mama later told me they disposed of the body in a dumpster at the Westown Shopping Center. I thought about Bear and the horrendous murder scene every time we went to the shopping center which was very often. I wonder if Mama thought about shooting at her daddy every time she went there as well.

I kept my distance from Keith as much as possible until he was later sent back to Alabama due to an unresolved case. I was ecstatic to hear that he would be out of our lives forever thanks to the judicial system. With Keith gone, Mama got a full-time job working second shift to support our family.

We moved into a three-bedroom ranch style house in the same neighborhood on Tyson Avenue. Reggie and I took advantage of Mama's late work hours and filled our house with the neighborhood boys and girls on any given day. Between his friends and mine, we always had an ample supply of marijuana and booze to party with. Deya spent most of her time at work, school or over a friends house.

A boy that used to frequent our house named Buster caught my eye. He lived around the corner and attended Patterson as well. I tasked my friend Akila with the responsibility of letting him know that I was interested. After her doing so, we flirted back and forth but he didn't approach me like I'd assumed he would. Weeks went by without him asking me out.

One day I was home alone watching music videos on Black Entertainment Television (BET). The doorbell rang and I pried myself off the couch to see who it was. Looking through the peephole, I saw a slim, dark skin, handsome male figure wearing a white t-shirt and khaki pants. It was my crush, Buster! He was alone in his school uniform with a bag of weed in his hand. Was this the moment I'd been waiting for? Was Buster about to ask me out? Exhilarated by a lustful desire, I opened the door and invited him inside.

"What's up Little Miss Thang? Your girl told me you was feeling me so what's up?" Buster kissed me on my lips, getting right to the reason behind his visit.

"Yeah and I be seeing you looking at me too." I admitted.

"Well shit, roll up and let's talk about it!" Buster handed me the bag of weed and a Swisher Sweet cigar. We sat down on our L-shaped sectional as I rolled the blunt up. Awkwardly making small talk and smoking, we watched music videos while giving each other googly eyes.

Once the weed was gone and we had nothing else to do with our hands, Buster and I found ourselves in a full on make out session. The music intensified the feelings of passion that was burning inside. "You gone let me hit it?" He whispered while softly rubbing me.

"Well if I do, what does that mean?" I challenged, hoping he would be my boyfriend.

"That means I'm yours and you mine." Buster assured me.

I hadn't had sex since that pregnancy scare with Cole a while back. I quickly weighed the options of being with Buster. He was handsome, athletic and came from a two-parent household. He had so much potential which excited me at the thought of being in a relationship with him.

"Where's your condom?" I inquired, insinuating that I was ready and willing to allow him into my pot of gold and solidify our new relationship.

"Damn, I left them at home. Give me two minutes and I'll be right back." Buster rushed out of the front door. I set the mood for what was going to be the first of many special moments with my new boyfriend. I cut the lights off, closed the curtains in the living room, turned the music up and lit a scented candle in my bedroom in preparation for our private, intimate exchange of energy.

Buster returned with the condoms in hand. "Oh yeah, this what I'm talking about!" He whispered, looking around the room at the ambiance I'd created.

"I'ma just pull the curtain back a little bit so we can see each other." He announced while kissing me. I thought that was a bit strange being that it wasn't pitch-black in the house, but ignored my suspicions being that I was easily manipulated. I stood up to escort him to my bedroom, but he sat down by the window and instructed me to come over to him.

"Oh my God, it's so wet!" Buster couldn't contain his pleasured state as we prematurely had sex. I heard whispering sounds coming from outside the living room window and jumped up off of him to see who it was. Surprisingly, it was three of his friends standing on my porch, laughing. They were looking through the opening of the window that Buster apparently created for us to put on a peep show.

"You dirty bastard!" I turned around to scold Buster for exposing our private moment and was appalled by the gruesome scene I was met with.

"Are you on your cycle?" He looked at me with a disgusted mug on his face. Blood was splattered all over his khaki pants, white t-shirt and hands. In fact, there was evidence on the carpet, table, walls and couch.

I'd heard stories about virgins having sex for the first time and her cherry popping. Although this wasn't my first time, it never happened to me before. Knowing that I wasn't on my menstrual cycle, I concluded that my cherry had just popped. Popping the cherry is slang for the breaking of the hymen which is inside of the vagina and can be broken with penetration, causing bleeding.

"No I'm not on my period, Stupid! Apparently you popped my cherry. Get the hell out of my house!" I snapped back with a disgusting look on my face, matching his.

"Do you have some clothes I can change into?" Buster asked as his face went from disgust to embarrassed.

"I should make your punk ass go out there just like this since you want to make a spectacle of yourself anyhow!" I was visibly infuriated.

"Come on, please Bridgett. I promise I didn't know they were out there." He lied to my face. Against my better judgement, I went to Reggie's room and got him a clean t-shirt but decided to make him leave in the blood splattered pants.

I gazed out of the window as Buster and his friends scurried away. They were laughing and pointing at his pants. Apparently, he never had any intentions of being my boyfriend. It was all part of a manipulative joke. According to Akila, I'd earned the nickname "Bloody Mary" at school and in the neighborhood.

The longing for love and belonging left me open to being easily manipulated. I wanted to be cool, be loved and to fit in but often found myself standing out. Feeling as if I was cursed, it seemed like God and everyone else I knew had turned their backs on me.

Have you ever felt that way? If so, know that before anyone could put a curse on you, God placed a blessing on you. He gave you power and dominion over all the earth. -*Genesis 1:26*. He didn't turn his back on me, just like He hasn't turned His back on you. He'll never put more on us than we can bear. I truly believe that God allowed me to make those mistakes so that in the future, they would bring glory and honor to His name.

He gave me the gift of public speaking, storytelling and writing so I could be of service and add value to those paralyzed by past mistakes, like I once was. Your unique story has a purpose. Once you begin to connect the dots, you'll uncover the treasure that was there all along. Allow the lessons to liberate you, knowing that you are set free through the blood of Jesus.

Although no one ridiculed me to my face, I disassociated myself from the reality of it all and began to skip school more often than before. When I did attend, my performance was poor under the influence of alcohol and marijuana. The school counselor later informed me that I had to attend summer school in order to be assigned to the 12th grade or else I'd have to repeat the 11th grade again.

Summer school at Belmont High School was an unexpected pleasantry. My friend Harmony was in attendance as well as a guy named Nathan from my neighborhood. I always knew he had a crush on me that persisted despite of the Bloody Mary incident that he knew all about. Nathan was around 5'4" with a scrawny frame accompanied by a miniature peanut sized head and small feet. His appearance instantly put him in the friend zone, but I never salvaged his hope by telling him that.

Nathan knew what it took to keep himself in my circle and really turned up the charm on the first day of summer school. "Hey Bridgett, I'm on probation so I can't smoke. Do you want this quarter pound of weed I got on me?" He asked while approaching Harmony and I outside of the building.

"Hell yeah, you know I do. How much?"

He pulled the bag of marijuana out of his backpack and slid it in the back pocket of my jeans. "It's free for you."

That noxious skunk resembling scent trailed alongside as I walked into the school, alarming everyone that I had illegal paraphernalia stashed somewhere on my person. Nathan, Harmony and I scouted the premises at lunch time, looking for a vacant classroom so we could smoke. All the summer school classes were held on the first floor. We figured any room on the second floor would suffice.

Rummaging through the hallway, tugging at each door, we found an opening to the perfect party central headquarters. We rationed that it must have been an English classroom due to the plethora of motivational posters plastered on all four walls. One of them stood out to me. It simply advertised the word T.H.I.N.K. It was an acronym used to think before you speak and ask yourself if what you are about to say is True. Honest. Inspiring. Necessary. Kind. We ignored the words of wisdom, opened the windows and proceeded to mix the conditioned air with cloudy weed smoke.

It wasn't too long before our lunchtime crew of three became a party of eight. Word got out amongst the students that I had weed and a secret hideout. I inadvertently became the Belmont summer school drug pusher.

After so long, I was beginning to feel guilty about profiting off the free weed from Nathan. Harmony then reminded me about a business lesson I seem to have forgotten. "What the hell do you feel guilty for? His dumb ass using the basics of supply and demand all wrong. He supplies you with weed and demands your time. You supply people with weed and demand their money. Everyone's getting what they want." She hit the blunt and continued. "Don't feel guilty, feel smart Bitch." That made sense to me, so I kept at it.

A couple weeks later, Nathan came to school with a fresh hit black eye. He confessed that he'd been stealing the marijuana from his stepdad in order to give to me. He was busted in the act the night before and they ended up brawling. Knowing that he turned into a petty thief and took a beating to appease me, I pulled him in close for a warm embrace. "Awwww you poor baby."

He melted right into the manipulative trap of my addiction. "You know I'll do anything for you."

I released myself from his desperate grip and pulled back to look him in the eye. "Well how am I going to get my weed now?"

With a blue and black eye socket, feeling sorry for me, he proudly announced "I got you girl. I'll just buy it from Ian in the neighborhood. He delivers." After one last gentle squeeze to assure him that I cared, the stoner crew and I finished smoking the rest of the weed left over from the last time Nathan robbed his stepdad.

We went back to class and attempted to pretend as if we were not under the influence of marijuana. I'm sure the teacher knew about our daily smoke fest. Every day after lunch, our relaxed eyes were bloodshot red and the classroom reeked of offensive skunk odor mixed with Morning Glory Body Mist. We were usually able to contain ourselves and not be a disturbance in class, but this day was different.

My desk was in the far back of the classroom. I was so high and out of my mind. It seemed like the teacher was up there performing a standup comedy routine. Everything she said was the funniest thing I'd heard all summer. "Alright class, who can read chapter 4 in the textbook for me?"

Looking over at Harmony, I slowly restated the joke out loud. "Did you hear that? She said who can read!" I chuckled while slapping myself on the knee.

Tears were jumping from my face and onto the desk, smearing the ink from the doodling I had done in my notebook. I laughed so hard that my stomach began to twist in knots. "My stomach hurts!" I cried aloud through the hysteria as the entire class laughed either with me or at me.

"Ms. Hatch, just go ahead and put your head down Baby." The teacher politely requested in a soft, nurturing tone.

Appreciative of her suggestion, I put my head down and robotically repeated after her in a nervous laughter, "She said just put your head down Ms. Hatch!"

Even with my head smothered into the folds of my arms on the desk, I couldn't contain myself. The violent laughter shook my entire body, moving the desk further back towards the window. I then felt a large object strike me on the crown of my head, making a clamorous sound and piercing the back of my neck before it made its way to the floor. "Ouch!" I muttered, disorientated and rubbing the back of my neck.

The students were laughing uproariously as I tried to figure out what just blew my high and slapped me sober. "What the hell was that?"

I took my hand from the back of my neck and examined it through blurry eyes. There was blood all over my hands and neck. "I'm bleeding!" I shrilled, hoping to cut into the amusement in the room.

"It was the fan!" Someone pointed out through their giggles. I looked on the floor to see the white square fan had fallen out of the window. It landed onto my head then cut me on the neck with one of the broken pieces on it's way down.

I felt a sense of relief knowing that I wasn't just attacked by an escapee from the Twin Valley Psychiatric Hospital that was down the street or that I wasn't just pistol whipped by a student trying to rob me for the weed money I'd just collected. "Are you ok Ms. Hatch?" The teacher interrupted my moment of gratitude.

I used the collar of my shirt to stop the bleeding and applied pressure to the back of my neck. "It's just a little cut. I'll be fine."

The teacher ordered the class to cease their disruptive laughter as she walked back to my desk with her hands clasped in front of her. Leaning in for a stronger impact, she whispered in my ear, "See, God don't like ugly." I gave her the greatest lip smack, head shake and eye roll that I could conjure up from the back of my bloody neck as she walked away.

After concluding that the teacher was accurate in her judgement of my ugliness, I put a stop to The Stoners Crew Lunchtime Smoke Fest after that day. Taking advantage of Nathan in order to feel a sense of love and belonging by others would come back to bite me in the butt a few years later. You'll read about that juicy story in Part III of "The First 33" book series, so be on the lookout!

Sometimes it takes a message from the universe, a wise counsel or a challenging situation to help us see things clearly. That fan knocking me upside the head was a wakeup call from God. I didn't need to sell weed to feel loved and important. Love was always right there within me. I was searching for something that I'd already possessed.

Could there be something you're looking for that God may have already given you the answer to? Could the answer be so simple or unconventional that you're overlooking it? I encourage you to be open, stay aware and look for messages and lessons in everything that occurs around you, to you and through you. Take mental notes and use them as you journey along in life, sharing the lessons with the ones you love. *"In vain have you acquired knowledge if you have not imparted it to others."* -Deuteronomy Rabbah, a homiletic commentary on the Book of Deuteronomy.

"There are six things the Lord hates, seven that are detestable to him: haughty eyes, a lying tongue, hands that shed innocent blood, a heart that devises wicked schemes, feet that are quick to rush into evil, a false witness who pours out lies and a person who stirs up conflict in the community." Proverbs 6:16-19 NIV

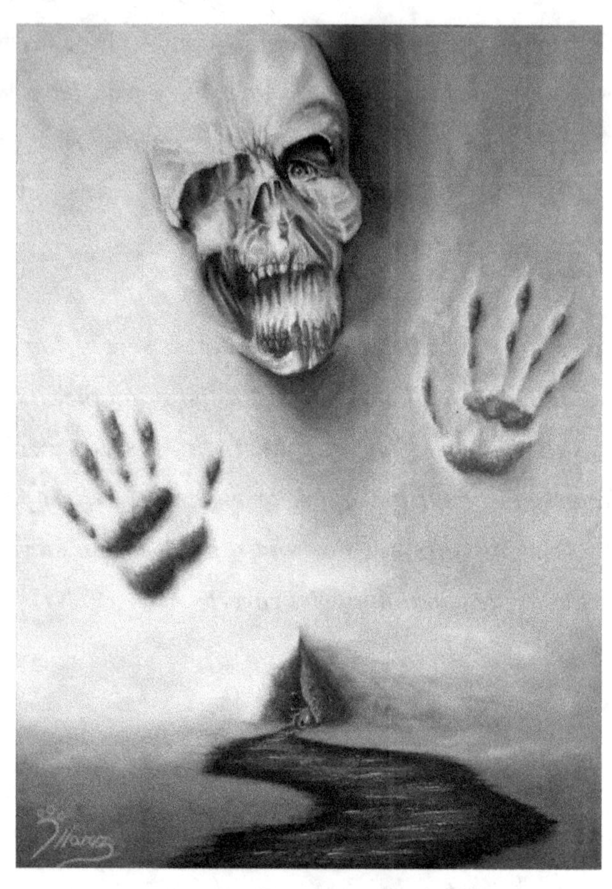

Marz Pacheco Original Art
"Una Riflessione" (A Reflection)
Los Angeles, CA

Chapter 6: Juvenile Behavior

Booty popping on a handstand was my favorite go to dance at the nightclubs. It usually attracted the male attention I craved but also came with the, "ugh what a nasty little skank," whispers that I despised from the girls. I decided to test my signature dance move at The Hot Boys concert to see if I could gain the attention of my celebrity crush, Juvenile.

The Dayton Memorial Hall was shoulder to shoulder packed with energized teenagers under the influence of God knows what, looking to get crunk and act up. DeNora and I centered ourselves right in front of the stage to be easily spotted by the famous rappers. Juvenile hit the stage going hard, *"Girl, you looks good, won't you back that azz up. You'se a big fine woman, won't you back that azz up. Call me Big Daddy when you back that azz up. Hoe, who is you playin wit? Back that azz up."*

The spirit of Jezebel must have washed over me or something. Although I had on white stockings, a white Tommy Hilfiger shirt and a matching jean skirt I'd stolen from the mall earlier that day, I dropped to the floor and introduced Juvie to my signature dance move. I'm booty popping on a handstand, DeNora two stepping and cheering me on, dudes in the crowd are looking, the girls turning up their noses but Juvenile wasn't paying me any attention.

"Bitch get up. He ain't even watching." DeNora tried to save face for me.

"That's alright, I'ma get his ass at the after party though!" I assured her while climbing up off the floor. I was convinced the stars had aligned for me to meet Juvenile well before the day of the concert. When Uncle Walt presented DeNora and I with two backstage passes he acquired for being head of security at the concert, I knew it was meant to be.

The after party was held downstairs in the Memorial Hall basement. Uncle Walt, his security team, the opening acts, a few others along with DeNora and I were awaiting The Hot Boys arrival. Birdman, Mannie Fresh, Young Turk, Lil Wayne and B.G. were some of The

Cashmoney Millionaires that were present but I only had eyes for Juvenile.

We enjoyed finger foods and alcohol beverages as I conversed with a guy I briefly dated before. He figured he'd shoot his shot once again, swearing that I was the one he let get away. "It's not by chance that we bumped into each other tonight. I knew I bought these backstage tickets for a reason!" He tried to convince me that I was the reason. "Let's go to the Waffle House and get some real food." He offered.

"Thanks but I came here for Juvenile and I am leaving here with Juvenile!" I affirmed with so much authority that I believed it myself.

"Oh I see. You on some groupie shit tonight. Just holla at me when he blows you off!" He walked away to try his Waffle House game on another girl.

The Hot Boys made their way to the after party causing an uproar throughout the crowd. I grabbed DeNora by the hand and we made our way over to Juvenile. He'd just finished posing for a picture with one of the opening act groups as we approached him.

"Juvie, come take a picture with me and my cousin!" I mouthed while grabbing him by his forearm.

"Get off of me!" He jerked his arm away. "Don't be putting your hands on me like that. You could have scratched me. How do I know if you got AIDS or not?" Juvenile yelled, causing all eyes to be on us.

"Forget you then! You wouldn't be shit without your fans. People like me who buy your album and keep you relevant!" I lied. Never had I bought an album from the store where it counts. My music came from the hustlers that hung out at the carwash on Gettysburg Ave. and sold bootleg tapes two for five dollars.

"Get up out of my face little girl. I ain't doing shit for you or your cousin now!" He ordered as his entourage began surrounding him, creating a barrier between the two of us.

"Forget you too! I'll have my uncle shut all this shit down you keep talking!" I threatened after Uncle Walt came over to see what all the ruckus was about.

In the middle of my speech, Juvenile proceeded to take his t-shirt off to expose his bulky muscles peeking through his white wife beater (undershirt). "If you don't get the hell away from me talking all that shit, we gone have some real problems here Wodie."

He followed up on his warning by spinning his t-shirt in the air above his head like a helicopter's blades, creating the force he needed to take off on me. The entourage strongly encouraged me to just walk away.

DeNora softly held me back as I pretended to run up to him swinging my fist, "I don't know who the hell you think you are but you got me all the way…"

My rant was abruptly interrupted. "Bridgett, calm down. Just leave the man alone!" Uncle Walt chimed in while gently grabbing me by the shoulders and escorting me away from Juvenile and his crew.

"Yeah that's right. Get that little girl out of here. It's your bedtime little Wodie!" He recited along with a few other lines that were thrown at me as I was pulled away waving both middle fingers in the air.

"Just stay away from him Bridgett. Don't get into no mess tonight." Uncle Walt ordered as he sat me down and walked off to continue securing the venue.

"Bitch you just got into it with Juvenile!" DeNora exclaimed.

"Forget him!" I yelled loud enough for everyone in the after party to hear me.

"Yeah you just keep your little ass over there!"
Juvenile yelled back.

The guy I briefly dated came over and reminded me that he was still available since I was blown off by Juvenile as he earlier predicted. I entertained him as a means to mitigate the misery I was feeling inside.

A while later, Juvenile and his crew walked towards us and his eyes were fixed in my direction. With a mean mug on my face, we locked eyes as he made an announcement, "Aye we about to bounce up out of here. Your loudmouth ass coming with me!" He bent down to get face to face with me, cringed up his nose and smirked as if we were just playing the entire time.

"Who me? I ain't going nowhere with you!" I snapped back, still sulking in embarrassment.

DeNora jumped in the middle of us, looked me in my eyes and shook me by the shoulders using all the seriousness she could muster up, "Bitch, we going with them!" Just then I remembered the reason why I went to the concert in the first place. I'd gotten what I wanted. It didn't come in the way that I imagined it but it did come true nonetheless.

"Alright let's go before I change my mind!", I responded, staying in character as a smart ass, which seemed to be foreplay to him.

We piled up in their limousine to take the short drive to the Doubletree Hotel downtown. "How old are you before we go any further?" Juvenile motioned for me to come and sit on his lap.

"Nineteen." I lied as I crawled over DeNora and the entourage to make my way to him. After landing on his lap, I swung my arm around his neck trying to be sexy.

"Degree needed!" Juvenile shouted in a thick, southern New Orleans dialect as everyone besides DeNora and I broke out in eye watering, knee slapping laughter.

DeNora and I didn't quite understand what he said at first but it slowly dawned on me once I'd gotten a whiff of my own underarm odor. All that dancing at the concert and after party left me sweaty and musty to a fault. Apparently, the Teen Spirit deodorant didn't do its job and Degree was needed. I continued to act like I didn't understand and left DeNora in the dark about what was so funny.

We arrived at the hotel, whispering and giggling about how much trouble we were going to get into once Uncle Walt realized we left with The Hot Boys. "Come in here with us Shawty, we about to chill and order a pizza." Young Turk invited DeNora inside the room with himself, B.G. and a few other guys.

I was hungry as well after only snacking on finger foods all night and went to follow behind her. Juvenile grabbed me by the arm stopping me at the door, "Where you going Wodie, we right here across the hall."

He slid the key card into the door and walked inside. "Oh shit! What am I doing? I don't want to have sex with the man, I just wanted to hang out with some celebrities for the first time." I thought while reluctantly walking into the room at the point of no return. I didn't think the situation through at all and I knew my provocative behavior was sending mixed signals.

An older man followed behind me along with another dude I recognized as one of the members of the entourage. Juvenile plopped down on the bed, grabbed the remote control and turned the channel to music videos on BET. "This is my dad and my cousin Duckdog." He said, calming my curiosity.

"How y'all doing?" I muttered falling into a deep and uncomfortable shyness, totally different from the girl they'd met at the after party. "We gone smoke this blunt then they gone leave." Juvenile explained while breaking down the Swisher Sweet, sprinkling the marijuana buds into it and rolling it up.

They laughed and joked in their thick New Orleans accent that I could barely comprehend besides the slang name Wodie, which they called everyone. I wasn't paying attention to them anyhow. I was contemplating my escape plan. I knew Juvenile was expecting me to back that azz up like his hit song said but I wasn't interested in being a hot girl that night. I was so intimidated!

"Alright Wodie, y'all know what time it is." Juvie sat up from the bed, hitting the blunt one last time before putting it out in the ashtray.

"I'ma leave these right here for you Wodie." His dad placed a pack of condoms on the nightstand.

"Nah we don't need those." Juvenile reported, handing them back to his father.

"Yeah we don't need those." I chimed in while getting up off the bed as well. "I'm about to go downstairs to the bar and have a drink." That was the only escape plan I could come up with in such a short time.

Duckdog and Juvenile's dad walked out of the room with me in tow right behind them. "I thought you was kicking it with me tonight!" Juvenile questioned.

"Nah, I'm going downstairs to the bar." I repeated, clearly not finding any other words to use.

"See I knew you had to be young. You ain't nineteen!" He challenged me.

I fought back using the only armor I had, my sassy mouth. "I am nineteen, what do I gotta lie to you for? Just cause I don't want to be in here with you don't mean I'm lying." I lied. Our familiar loud disturbance caused Young Turk to open his door across the hall. DeNora stepped out munching on a slice of pizza. I wanted some.

"Aye man, bring me two bitches upstairs!" Juvenile mouthed into the receiver of his cellular phone while looking at me. Everyone stood in the hallway as he and I taunted one another until his homeboy got off the elevator with two beautiful women by his side. "I had two titties, now I got four!" Juvie placed his arms around the girls, escorting them into his luxury suite that was once occupied by my sweet 16-year-old ignorance.

"Come on Bitch, he's tripping!" I explained to DeNora while grabbing her hand to walk away.

"Nah, y'all cool. Just go in there and chill with Turk and nem'." Juvenile suggested as he gave me a playful snarky look while shutting his door to entertain his four titties. We did just as he said and chilled with The Hot Boys until the public transportation resumed in the morning, then made our way to the bus stop.

A few months later, Juvenile came back to Dayton, OH to perform at the Ervin J. Nutter Center. Knowing that they stayed at the Doubletree Hotel when they came into town, I convinced my friend Akila to skip school and go to the hotel with me. I assured her they would remember who I was and we'd be granted the privilege of going to the concert with them. Akila and I were a lot alike so I knew she'd be down for the cause. She was a short, brown skin, cute, loud, raving ball of fire with a huge "screw the world personality" who loved to drink, smoke and have a good time.

When we arrived at the hotel, we were greeted by the front desk concierge lady. We didn't realize that it was her job to greet us and ask how she could help. I thought she recognized that we were just some kids skipping school, so I lied using my grown-up voice. "Um yes, I'm looking for my friend Terrence who works here. Do you know what floor he's on please?" That was partly true. I did know a guy named Terrence that worked there but I wasn't looking for him.

Akila glanced over at me with an impressed grin as the concierge contemplated who Terrence was. "Terrence, oh yes. I believe he's on the 4th floor. Should I tell him you're here?"

"No thanks, we'll find him!" I answered as the two of us locked arms and skipped over to the elevators, giggling.

We scurried down the halls on a few different floors, listening at each door to hear if the Cashmoney crew were in there. Once we made our way to the 8th floor, we walked head on into two young black men who were iced out with diamond watches, bracelets and earrings. One of them had a Cashmoney Records medallion around his neck. Akila pinched the fat on the back of my arm in excitement, "Bitch we found them!"

"What's up Shawties?" The handsome brown skin, short, stalky one with the Cashmoney chain and braided hair slyly greeted us as they were walking by.

"Aye where Juvenile at?" Akila blurted out causing the two of them to stop and look back at us.

The other guy was slightly older with light skin, a bald head and a slick mouth. "What are you gonna do for us if we tell you? You got to take care of the gatekeepers too now Wodie!"

I thought Akila was about to curse him out, but she surprised me with her flirty and playful energy. "Nah, my friend already knows them. Bridgett kicks it with Juvenile every time y'all come to town!" She repeated what I exaggerated and told her.

"Do one of y'all braid hair?" Dude with the braids questioned.

"Akila does and she's the coldest in the city!" I vouched.

"Bet! Come to our room and get me fresh then I'll get you two in the concert and backstage tonight." He promised. We followed them to their room. They poured us some drinks and we smoked a few blunts while Akila braided dudes' hair.

Wodie with the bald head excused himself so he could get ready for the concert. "Aye yo Shawty, come here real quick", he yelled from the bathroom. Akila and I looked at one another like who is he talking to.

"Go see what Wodie talkin bout Shawty. He cool people, he ain't gone do nothing to you." Reluctantly listening to Wodie with the braids, I opened the bathroom door and found Dude sitting in the bathtub covered in bubbles which made him look a lot less threatening.

"Close the door and come wash my back for me real quick." I silently stood at the door as he stroked himself while probing me to join in.

"Do you want to do it?" He offered, pointing his intimidating manhood in my direction. I shook my head no and simply walked out and shut the door behind me without mumbling a word.

Once Akila finished braiding Wodie's hair, we walked back to school in time to catch the bus home and got cute for the concert. Akila's mom dropped us off at the Ervin J. Nutter Center thinking that I'd won concert tickets on the radio. We found our way to the backstage door entrance and called Wodie with the braids. After numerous attempts to contact him to no avail, it dawned on us that we were on our own.

Just our luck, some men opened up the door to come outside and smoke. We told them we were a part of Juvenile's entourage and had gotten locked out. They allowed us to come in with no questions asked. We made our way backstage to the VIP lounge. Wodie with the braids was quite startled once he saw us.

"Aye, y'all made it!" He faked an excited cheer over the ear-splitting acoustics.

"Yeah, no thanks to you!" I acknowledged. He lied of course, talking about he couldn't answer the phone because it was too loud and he didn't hear it ringing and blah blah blah.

"Okay well I mean, I braided your hair for free and you promised us we'd be able to hang out with Juvenile nem' so what's up?" Akila challenged.

"Okay, I tell y'all what. Meet me at the hotel as soon as the concert is over and I'll make sure that y'all get in the after party. It's going down in our room!" He assured us.

After enjoying ourselves and turning up at the concert, we hitched a ride to the Doubletree Hotel and

Wodie with the braids actually answered his phone. We tried our best to hide our childish excitement once entering the room amongst all the Hot Boys. Juvenile, Lil Wayne, Birdman, Mannie Fresh and their crew were partying and talking in their thick New Orleans accent that I loved so much.

There were a few other girls in the room sitting quietly and being pretty. Akila broke the ice, speaking loudly over the music, demanding all eyes on her. "Hey everybody!   I'm Akila and this is my best friend Bridgett!" She then looked over at Juvenile to remind him of who I was, "Aye Juvie, you remember Bridgett don't you? She kicked it with you last time y'all was here!"

"Nah, I don't even know Shawty. I meet so many people on tour, why would I remember her?"

Embarrassed and desperate to be relevant and remembered, I calmly refreshed his memory. "Well, I was the girl who went to the hotel room with you, your dad and your cousin Duckdog. I didn't want to stay so you told your security guard to bring you two girls." Remember you said, "I had two titties, now I got four?"

Laughing at the thought of himself saying that, Juvie responded, "Oh yeah, I do remember you, I do." I doubt if he did.

We popped bottles as weed smoke filled the room and bodies dripped of sweat from all the bumping and grinding on the dance floor. Akila grabbed one of the Hot Boys and started backing that azz up on him. Juvenile wanted in on the action and pulled me close to dance with him. Thank God I'd switched from Teen Spirit to Degree, it did me justice.

He was drinking out of a huge bottle of Hennessy as I slowly grinded in front of him. The next thing I know, a hard, heavy cold object swiftly made contact with my forehead, sending me to a crouched position on my knees while soothing myself. I looked up to see Juvenile holding the fifth of Hennessy in one hand and the other hand over his mouth in amazement. "My bad Shawty. I didn't mean to do that!" He apologized as he extended his hand to help me stand upright.

"It's all good, I know you didn't mean it." I tried to convince myself through the chuckles of everyone in the room. At the back of my mind, I wondered if it was really an accident or did he hit me in the head to get back at me for playing him the last time we met? It also could have been God knocking some sense into me again like He did with that fan in summer school! Either way, I brushed it off and refilled my cup.

Lil Wayne got up from the couch and was about to leave. Akila decided it was time for him to hit the dance floor as well. "Let's sandwich him! I'll get the front, you get the back!" She stopped him before making his way to the door.

"Oh no, no, no. My baby momma upstairs." He shut us down real quick. His baby momma Toya was upstairs in their hotel room with their daughter Reginae. Both are now Reality TV stars amongst other things. I remember thinking, "Wow he's so young and respectable."

The party began to wind down and it was time for us to vacate the premises. Akila was passed out on the bed with the red cup gripped tightly in her hand. "Aye yo, wake Shawty up Ma!" Some dude demanded then announced to the rest of the party. "Aye we got flights to catch so if you not with the Cashmoney Millionaires then you got to go!" Juvenile's dad was really sweet like the last time I'd met him. He inquired about how we were getting home. I fabricated a story that Akila's sister was on her way to pick us up.

Akila and I hung out in the hotel lobby drinking complimentary coffee until sunrise. We staggered downtown to the bus stop trying to look as sober as possible. We were approached by a handsome older gentleman of average height, average built with a single dimple on his left cheek and a bright welcoming smile, wearing a brown leather jacket. "Where y'all going looking so fine this early in the morning?" He inquired. Akila sat down at the bus stop and closed her eyes while I indulged in conversation with him.

The man introduced himself as Cain. After talking for a while, he offered to take us home. I was down to hop in the car with the stranger but Akila had more sense. She knew better than doing something so stupid and dangerous like that and demanded we get on the bus together.

Cain and I exchanged numbers after agreeing to link up later in the week. To my surprise, he invited me to accompany him to his 30th birthday party the next week. I couldn't believe the man was 30. He didn't look a day over 21. I didn't want to be by myself with all his older and sophisticated friends, so I invited my friend Latrice to join us.

Latrice attended the same high school as Akila and I. She was a very well-mannered young lady, always saying, Yes Ma'am and No Sir to her elders which made a great impression on the old folks. Her shy, good girl demeanor was very deceiving though. No, she didn't smoke weed or drink alcohol but Latrice loved her some boys and was someone I could always count on to skip school, laugh and have fun with.

Cain had his 30th birthday party at the K-9 Club. We met all of his family and friends who seemed to have loved the people we pretended to be, which were 20 year old college graduates from The University of Dayton. Cain said it was best for me to lie about my age so his family didn't think I was too immature for him. Latrice had fun putting on an act but she wasn't into older men and was ready to go. We both had Daddy issues, but she liked her dudes young, dumb and full of...fun.

After the party, Cain and I dropped Latrice off at home then went to his aunt's house. He gave me a tour of the modest, ranch style, three-bedroom home. When we got to his little cousin's room, I noticed a huge Barney poster on the wall and instantly got excited. "Oh my God, I love Barney!" I exclaimed.

"You get that excited when you see Barney?" He grimaced.

"I was being sarcastic Silly. That show drives me crazy with all them mushy songs!" I exaggerated, knowing that I adored Barney and still watched it at home from time to time. The songs were very mushy though.

Cain then took me to another bedroom, "And this is my room." He announced.

"You live with your aunt?" Now I was the one with a grimace on my face, feeling bamboozled. I assumed he had his own place.

"Yeah, she's a single mom. I'm just staying here to help her out with the bills." At the time, that was totally believable. I later learned that was a manipulation tactic some men used when they were shy about not having their own place. Cain did his best to seduce me that night only to find out that I was still a virgin. At least that's what I told him, figuring I'd stay in lying mode for the night.

Cain and I started spending a lot of time together. Just as I began to contemplate on making him my man, the foolishness set in motion and I realized how badly he desired to be with a virgin. He started paging my beeper frequently, excessively calling my house phone and professing his undying love for me on the daily. I was bumping into him at all the places I frequented. The mall, downtown, my neighborhood stores and the clubs. The stalking tendencies were confirmation that it was high time I broke things off with him.

It had been two weeks since I cut all ties with Cain and he'd apparently ceased with the obsessive behavior. Then one day, my brother and I were chilling at home when we heard a thunderous crashing sound followed by glass shattering outside of his bedroom window. Afraid that someone threw a brick at our house in an attempt to break in, we moved away from the windows and called the police to report our suspicions. Once the officers arrived, they searched the premises and identified the object thrown as a framed Barney poster.

Knowing very well that it was the same Barney Poster from Cain cousin's bedroom, I was petrified but couldn't bring myself to confess that I was being stalked and taunted by a 30-year-old man. The police credited it to some unruly teens in the neighborhood, but I knew the truth. It wasn't a teen that did this, but a grown man named Cain who exhibited juvenile behavior.

This incident only increased the level of mistrust that I carried from my early years. It communicated to me in essence, that I couldn't allow anyone to get too close. If so, they would require more than I was willing to give, then obsessively seek after my attention like Cain. I would later go throughout life carrying that story alongside me like an old beat up teddy bear. From relationship to friendship to the therapist couch.

If you can relate and are holding on to a story that you've hauled from the past to the present, it would behoove you to quickly change the narrative. We hear a lot about forgiveness these days and how we have to forgive ourselves for the mistakes we've made in order to move on. Let me tell you, I tried that and it didn't work. I kept affirming to myself in the mirror that I forgive you Bridgett for this and that and the other, but the penetrating feeling of doom, guilt and self-pity was overwhelmingly hovering over me yet and still.

It wasn't until I volunteered to be on the leadership team at GAP Community's transformation conference, "Awaken", that I realized I didn't have to forgive myself for the mistakes of my past (visit www.gapcommunity.com for more information).

One day at our team meeting, I questioned Jean-Marie Jobs, the founder of GAP Community and Nathan Neighbor, Humanity Church Pastor, about self-forgiveness. I shared how I was trying so hard to forgive myself for past mistakes, but the shameful feelings would continuously creep up here and there.

Jean-Marie and Nathan brought to my attention that nowhere in the Bible does God instruct us to forgive ourselves. Forgive, is what we do when others wrong us, not ourselves. The Word talks a lot about forgiving others as many as seventy-seven times according to Matthew 18: 21-22 NIV which reads, "Then Peter came to Jesus and asked, "Lord, how many times shall I forgive my brother or sister who sins against me? Up to seven times?" Jesus answered, "I tell you, not seven times, but seventy-seven times."

Jesus already paid the penalty for each individual's sin in order to right the relationship between God and humanity, a relationship damaged by sin. Jesus's death on the cross is the penalty or "satisfaction" for sin. So you see, we are already forgiven. I learned that it was my responsibility to ACCEPT forgiveness for myself and that changed the game! "Be kind and compassionate to one another, forgiving each other, just as in Christ God forgave you." -Ephesians 4:32 NIV

I reiterate, if you are holding on to shame, embarrassment or guilt due to the sins of your past, confess it and accept that you are already forgiven because Jesus died for you, knowing that you knew not what you were doing. You were exhibiting juvenile behavior from which you are already forgiven. Let it go and free yourself because as Lena Horne said, *"It's not the load that breaks you down, it's the way you carry it."*

 "When I was a child, I talked like a child, I thought like a child, I reasoned like a child. When I became a man, I put the ways of childhood behind me." 1 Corinthians 13:11 NIV

Richard Martinez

"Change The Tape"

Newport, CA

Chapter 7: Stop Digging...You Are Treasure

The feeling of being unprotected was a major driving force in my decision to date who I thought was one of the city's biggest drug dealers. I met Ian when he delivered some marijuana to my house for Akila. He rolled up in a midnight blue, old school Chevy with bloody red, crushed velvet interior and a stereo system so powerful that it shook our house windows as he pulled into the driveway.

"Bitch who is that?" I inquired, being fully sucked in by his thirst trapping vehicle.

"Oh that ain't nobody by Ian's freaky ass. He be trying to holla at everybody." She warned.

We hopped in his car and just like she predicted, Ian turned on his charm. "How you doing, Miss Chocolate Drop? Where you been hiding all my life?"

"It don't matter where I've been, all that matters is

where I'm going." I mischievously shot back.

"Oh a feisty one! I can dig it!" He grinned.

"Man, forget all that. Where the weed at?" Akila chimed in, visibly annoyed by our playful banter.

As Ian reached into his glove compartment to withdraw his weed, I noticed a handgun along with stacks of money that piqued my interest. I developed a preference for men with guns being that I felt like someone was always out to get me. Plus, he was tall, dark and handsome, most girls dream man.

Ian and I exchanged numbers and were quickly inseparable. All I ever wanted was a man to spoil me but when Ian took me to the mall and said, "You can have whatever you like, no limits," I didn't even know where to begin. My idea of being spoiled was unlimited weed and alcohol. As far as the mall went, the heights that my immature mind leaped to was only clothes and gym shoes. I walked right past the jewelry stores without a second thought. The biggest incentive for having Ian as a boyfriend was that I no longer had to go half on a dime bag of weed.

Ian didn't have to do too much to impress my mama and dad either. Mama liked him simply because he knew how to charm women. When Ian and my dad first met, I thought there was going to be some type of gun play. My dad came to visit after his shift at the Dayton Correctional Institute where he was a correctional officer. Upon introducing Ian to him as my boyfriend, my dad took it upon himself to casually show Ian his firearm. That then sparked a conversation about guns. To my bewilderment, Ian popped his trunk, revealing a collection of shotguns, rifles and handguns stashed in a duffle bag. I thought my dad would be appalled that his daughter was with a man of that caliber, but he was unmistakably impressed by the metal.

"What you doing riding around like that, Man? You better put them guns up before you get caught slipping." Dad expressed tenderly.

Ian then opened the door, reached to the back of his old school Ford Mustang and pulled out two extra large trash bags full of weed. He welcomed my dad to peak his head inside. "I got to protect what's mine by all means."

"Alright as long as you take care of my daughter. That's all I care about." Dad approved, after asking for and receiving some weed.

Ian could do no wrong when it came to my parents, unfortunately, that was far from the relationship his mom and I shared. Although he actually paid all of the bills, Ian still lived in his mother's house. She was an avid fan of the Soap Opera, "The Bold and the Beautiful." One of the fictional characters on the show named Brooke was apparently a home wrecker who had a daughter named Bridget. She would often tell me that my mama should have named me Brooke instead of Bridgett because I was turning her home into a whore house.

My only comeback to her insults was, "Whatever, my man pays all the bills in this house so I ain't going nowhere!" She couldn't stand me so much that she despised my smile. She often ordered me to "put that smile up" as I walked into the house, especially if her man was there. After months of petty bickering with his mom, I encouraged Ian to move out on his own and he did. He found a small one -bedroom apartment in the Westwood/Roosevelt area. Finally, we could do what grown folks did in peace without his mother banging on the ceiling, ordering us to quiet down.

This area, like many areas on the west side of Dayton, had a high crime rate. I wasn't frightened until one of Ian's cars was stolen from right in front of the apartment while we were sleeping. He didn't try to hide the fact that he was what some might call, "hood rich." People saw his collection of classic cars and someone obviously decided to take one for themselves.

Ian and his brother set out to look for the car after reporting it stolen to the police. I begged him not to leave me alone, fearing the thieves would come back to rob the place, but he left me anyhow. I found myself hiding under the covers in the dark, eating a ham and cheese sandwich, clutching onto a butcher's knife and anticipating an altercation.

That was the moment I realized Ian couldn't provide me with the type of protection I'd been longing for. What I didn't know was that I was already protected by the blood of Jesus and was looking for refuge under a man's wings when God was my shield and my fortress. It would take many years, mistakes and lessons before I could understand that truth.

The police later found his vehicle abandoned in a park, stripped of it's 24" rims, stereo system and everything else of value. After that night, something inside of Ian had snapped, causing him to grow suspicious of everything and everyone around him, especially me. His first peculiar act was placing a padlock on the refrigerator. He rarely had company at his place and when he did, nobody went in the refrigerator but he and I.

When I questioned him about the lock, he stated that someone kept eating up all his ham and cheese and he was sick of it. We both knew that the someone he was referring to was me. From then on, he started picking fights with me about any minute thing. I endured his abrupt change of behavior until it all took a major turn for the worse.

Ian had been gone all day. I was at his apartment blowing his phone up, fearing that something bad happened to him. He finally came home and blatantly ignored me, sat on the couch then gazed into the darkness of the television screen.

"Babe, is everything ok? You seem upset." I surmised while taking a seat next him and placed my hand on his thigh.

"Get your hoe ass off of me!" He raged then jumped up off the couch and into my face.

"What the hell Ian!" I clapped back.

"Do you know who Jabari is?" He interrogated.

"I don't know him personally but I heard he was making big moves in the city, just like you." I remarked contemptuously.

"Stop lying Bitch! I just met up with him and asked did he know a girl named Boo. Guess what he said?" He tested me.

"Bitch?" I jumped up off the couch and into his face. I'm not going to be another Bitch, Ian! I'm pretty sure I'm not the only girl in the city with the nickname, Boo!" I reasoned. "Are you accusing me of cheating on you with Jabari?"

"He said he's been messing around with you for two months now! I showed him your picture! I knew I should have listened to my mama!" He was bawling and hysterical at this point. With tears of rage, Ian darted out of the door.

"Ian! Stop! Come back!" I wailed, matching his hysterical state of being.

Ignoring my cries, he jumped into his most prized classic car and sped off driving recklessly up the street. I ran to my mama's car that I borrowed and followed him up Third Street, one of the busiest streets in the city. He carelessly swerved from lane to lane at about 80mph with me closely in tow. He made his way to the intersection of Third and Gettysburg and made a startling stop. Cars were speeding by and honking their horns, signaling for him to get out of the way.

Instead of moving, Ian parked his car in the intersection, turned the engine off and got out of his vehicle. He opened the back door and pulled out a 12 pack of Budweiser. Snapping them off the plastic holder one by one, he passed the cans out to motorists as they drove by, professing that he was Moses and Jesus was coming back soon! I was bawling and pleading for him to get out of the busy traffic but my desperate cries landed on deaf ears. Flabbergasted, I couldn't think of what to do. Fearing I'd get Ian in major trouble or shot dead, I didn't dare call the police, especially since he usually had guns and weed on him. I sped off to Ian mom's house to see if his brother could talk some sense into him.

When we pulled up to the scene, Ian's car was no longer in the intersection. It was parked on the corner of Gettysburg Ave., surrounded by four police cruisers, one of which Ian was handcuffed in the back seat. His brother and I proceeded to walk up to the cruiser as Ian was calmly talking to an officer through the window. As soon as he seen me, he was triggered again. "Noooooo! Don't let her come near me! She's going to kill me! She killed like three of her boyfriends already and I'm next!" He desperately rioted.

Totally alarmed by his preposterous accusations and not wanting any personal dealings with the police, I quietly turned to walk back to the car and allow Ian's brother to handle it from there. "Ma'am, can I see some identification please?" The officer asked as if it was a request and not a demand.

"Ummm my ID is ummmm…" Looking through my purse, I stalled while contemplating on whether or not I should use my friend Latrice's name since I didn't have a valid driver's license and I was on probation for stealing!

"Her name is Bridgett LaRé Hatch. She's a 5'4" murderer with black hair, brown eyes, she lives at…," Ian continued snitching until his brother calmed him down. Being that they knew my real name, I retrieved my identification from my purse and hesitantly handed it to the officer while defending my honor.

"I am in no way a murderer. I shared with him that a couple of my ex-boyfriends were murdered by the streets, but he knows I didn't have anything to do with it. I don't know what's going on with him!" I confessed.

"Thank you Ma'am. You mind having a seat while I run this in the system real quick, just to be sure?" He asked while opening up the back door to his cruiser.

"Yes I do mind!" I rejected his offer. "I haven't done anything wrong for you to place me in a cruiser. You can run my name while I stand right here on this sidewalk. I ain't going nowhere!" I forcefully suggested.

He tasked another officer with keeping an eye on me until he returned. Ian was laughing and talking with his brother when he looked over at me and winked his eye, clearly impressed with the dismay he was causing.

"Alright Ma'am. Everything came back clean." The officer stated as he gave me my ID.

"I told you I wasn't no damn murderer!" I reminded him.

The officers informed Ian's brother and I that they were taking him to the county jail and towing his vehicle. When we got to their mom's house, I was scolded with accusations that my demonic spirit literally drove her baby insane. Not willing to disrespect her and too worn out to engage in any further confrontation, I walked out without incident.

A few days later I got a call from Ian informing me that he believed someone laced his marijuana with some type of psychotropic chemical, causing him to act the way in which he did. When I questioned him on his whereabouts, he reported that he'd been admitted to Twin Valley Psychiatric Hospital and pleaded for me to come and visit him. I enlisted my mama to accompany me for moral support. I knew she would have my back if he tried anything because she was all about the drama when it came to her children.

To my surprise, Ian greeted us with a huge joyful smile, warm hugs and kisses. He appeared to be extremely happy and carefree as he gave us a tour of his temporary new home. When we got to his room, he apologized for the pain he may have caused me and joked about the look on my face when he told the police I was a murderer. I still didn't think it was funny, but I giggled anyhow. Mama was braiding his hair when an orderly came in to deliver the news that he had another visitor.

Ian jumped up with glee as a young man walked in with a suitcase in his hand. I recognized him from the television commercials for Gold 4 Ya Mouth, a company that customized gold teeth and grills to put on your teeth. He was there to get a molding for Ian's customized grill that he'd ordered.

I took a step back and analyzed the situation. I'm a 17-year-old student visiting my boyfriend in a psychiatric facility. Mama up in here braiding his hair and he's being fitted for gold teeth while other patients come in and out the room to visit like they were having a slumber party.

Ian was very comfortable with taking a break from reality at the psychiatric facility. After weeks of visiting him, I felt like a patient as well. I wasn't religious or spiritual at the time, but I decided to have a conversation with "the God" I'd heard Grandma Jewel's pastor speak about when I used to go to church with her as a child. I concluded I was too young to be in the predicament that I was in and decided to end the relationship with Ian once he was released from the hospital. The initial pain of the breakup was torture, but we were able remain cordial being that we shared a network of friends.

The overwhelming desire to be loved, protected and provided for hijacked my confidence and seized my youth like a hostile parasitic fungi invasion. The vicious cycle of aimlessly seeking refuge under a man's arms was my neutral way of being. I didn't understand that there was only one source which was the master key to everything my heart desired...God is the source!

Have you ever heard the cliche, "All that glitters ain't gold?" I was digging for someone to be my pot of gold, only to find out that I carried the treasure within me all along. The God in me is Treasure. I didn't comprehend that God is love (John 4:16). I didn't understand that God is Jehovah Jireh, my provider (Genesis 22:8). I didn't fathom that the Lord is my refuge and fortress and will protect me (Psalm 91).

If you are a woman in hot pursuit of love and protection like I was, then this message is for you. A woman's instinctive desire to feel protected by a man is a hard-wired, feminine instinct that goes all the way back to the beginning of humanity's history. It's natural for loving, soft feminine energy to seek the protection of masculine energy, whether it's opposite or same sex relationships. It's the law of polarity.

A girl's father is usually the first to provide her with this need. When that isn't the case, some of us are misguided in our pursuit but that doesn't mean we're gold diggers as some like to term it as a shame tactic. We are Treasure Hunters! Sometimes treasures are deeply buried in the disappointments of the past. You have to do the work and dig deep to uncover it.

When you expose the treasure; the core of your being, weed out the counterfeit and keep what is authentic to you. Then when you do pray for that which you desire, pray in explicit detail and believe that God's will for your life will be done. As Dr. Maya Angelou said, *"Your life is much more important than you can imagine...it is your first treasure."* You are Treasure!

"Whoever dwells in the shelter of the Most High will rest in the shadow of the Almighty. 2 I will say of the Lord, "He is my refuge and my fortress, my God, in whom I trust." 3 Surely he will save you from the fowler's snare and from the deadly pestilence. 4 He will cover you with his feathers, and under his wings you will find refuge; his faithfulness will be your shield and rampart. 5 You will not fear the terror of night, nor the arrow that flies

by day, 6 nor the pestilence that stalks in the darkness, nor the plague that destroys at midday. 7 A thousand may fall at your side, ten thousand at your right hand, but it will not come near you. 8 You will only observe with your eyes and see the punishment of the wicked. 9 If you say, "The Lord is my refuge," and you make the Most High your dwelling, 10 no harm will overtake you, no disaster will come near your tent. 11 For he will command his angels concerning you to guard you in all your ways; 12 they will lift you up in their hands, so that you will not strike your foot against a stone. 13 You will tread on the lion and the cobra; you will trample the great lion and the serpent.14 "Because he loves me," says the Lord, "I will rescue him; I will protect him, for he acknowledges my name. 15 He will call on me, and I will answer him; I will be with him in trouble, I will deliver him and honor him. 16 With long life I will satisfy him and show him my salvation." Psalm 91 NIV

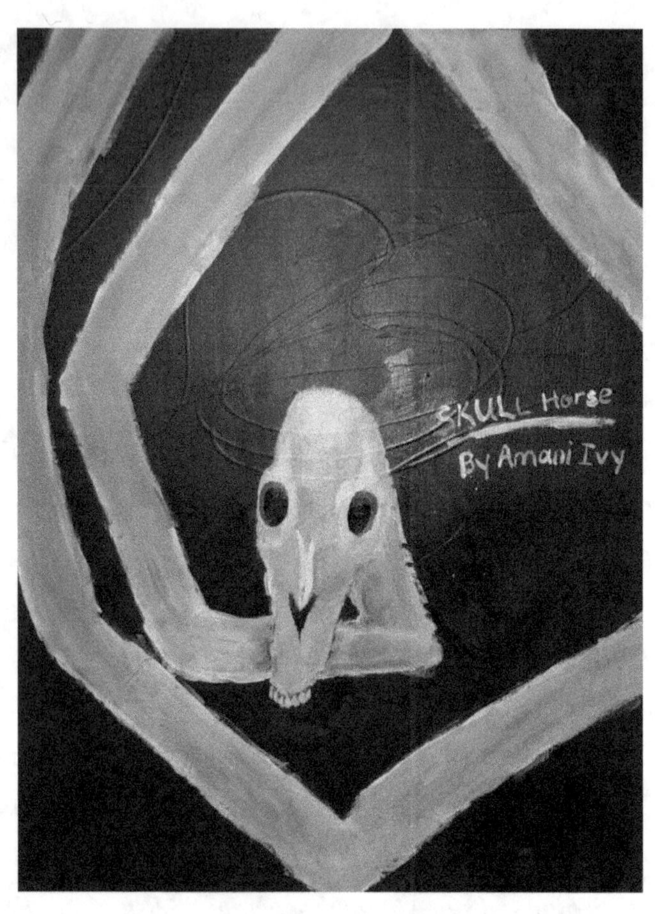

Art by Amani Ivy

"Skull Horse"

Dayton, OH

Chapter 8: Jab, Cross, Jab, Cross

Doing no more than the bare minimum, I made it all the way to senior year. An overwhelming desire to actually graduate from high school overtook me and I couldn't take any chances on failing. For the first time in a long time, the teachers saw me in class every day. I still wasn't what you'd call a model student to say the least. Every morning I showed up loudly reeking of marijuana and Newport cigarettes.

The principal, Mrs. Vapor, was on the younger side of her 40's I believe. When my teachers would send me to her office, she'd make me chill with her on lunch duty. In the lunchroom, I'd soothe my desire for snacks and chat with her about various topics. She was often curious about who I did and didn't like and why. I remember her asking me about a particular teacher whom

I thought despised my friends and I because we often smelled like weed.

"I can't stand that bitch. She always looks at me funny." The face I displayed mocked the teacher.

Principal Vapor laughed at my level of disgust and shared what she knew about her. "You know, I heard she hangs out with these little boys after school hours. Do you know anything about that?"

"That's not surprising. I haven't heard anything but the way she dresses, I wouldn't put a past to it." Principal Vapor giggled at my referencing the teacher, dressing like a teenager.

Shortly after Principal Vapor shared her suspicions, Akila and I were walking downtown after school, when that same teacher pulled up on us. "Hey, y'all need a ride?"

"No thanks." We naturally declined and shared a look of confusion.

The teacher insisted, "Come on, get in the car. I'm going y'all way anyhow."

At this point, I thought she'd heard about the rumor Principal Vapor shared and wanted to interrogate me or something. I held up the blunt so she could see it. "We got something to take care of real quick."

"Whatever, just get in the car girls!" The teacher demanded.

Akila and I looked at each other in suspense of her motives. I whispered in her ear what I'd heard and Akila perceived that the teacher wanted to smoke with us. Out of curiosity, we obeyed and got in the car. I hopped in the front and instantly tested Akila's discernment.

"So I can smoke in here right?" I assessed her standards while putting the blunt in my mouth and flicking the lighter.

"Girl what makes you think you can smoke in my car. I can't be seen with some rebellious teenagers smoking weed!" She surprised us with that answer.

"Oh well shoot, you can take us back to the bus stop because we already showed you what we was about to do. School is out!" Akila snapped.

"Calm down girl! I'm going to stop by my house and grab something real quick." She asserted. Akila and I shared an apprehensive expression, but said nothing.

We arrived at the teachers home and instead of her just grabbing something, she invited us to come inside.

"So can I spark it up now?" I pleaded after she proudly gave us a tour of her home.

"Alright, go ahead but don't tell y'all little friends. I don't like those other girls y'all be hanging out with. They talk too much." That explained the snarky looks she would give us in the hallway that led me to tell Principal Vapor I couldn't stand her.

After agreeing to keep her little secret, Akila and I smoked with the teacher quite frequently at either her house or mine. If ever her friends or family came over, we had the privilege of pretending to be college graduates, whom she was mentoring. We thought it was so cool that we were hanging out and influencing a teacher to be a bad girl, smoking and drinking with us. The public school system was always a joke as far as I was concerned.

Assuming I wouldn't fail my senior year because of my advantage with the teacher and principal, I fell back into my ways of frequently skipping out on class. One day, Akila, Latrice and I left school with two of the more popular girls to hang out downtown. One of the girls,

Olivia, invited her boyfriend to meet us there. He showed up with a quarter bag of weed and smoked us out on the rooftop of one of the commercial buildings we frequented. Her boyfriend was quite friendly with all of us girls but not in a flirty way. He was just a really cool dude that apparently liked to hear himself talk. We all had a fun time and then went our separate ways, so I thought.

The next day at school, Olivia and I were walking in opposite directions of the hallway. "Hey Girl!" I happily exclaimed, thinking we were fast friends since yesterday.

"Move Bitch!" She responded with a shove of her elbow, knocking me into the lockers. I was dumbfounded on what the hostility was all about, but at that point, I didn't care.

"What the hell is wrong with you?" I shot back as another classmate held me back and inquired about what happened. Olivia kept walking down the hall and didn't turn around or stop to appease my curiosity. "I don't know what her problem is but I didn't do anything to her!"

The charades with Olivia went on for the rest of the week without an explanation as to why she was bullying me. She'd bump into me in the hallway, talk poorly behind my back and appointed various friends of hers to taunt me on site as well. Subsequently, I was on my way to the lunchroom to hang out with Principal Vapor and spotted Olivia walk into the bathroom by herself. I followed her into the stall. "Ok, what exactly is your problem with me? If you want to fight then let's go right here, right now!" I challenged as she was bent over to pull her pants down.

"Oh no! Un un! Let me out of here! Watch out!" She expressed while lightly brushing past me to exit the stall, walked out of the bathroom and into the hallway as I followed behind her. Olivia walked far enough down the hall until she met with one of her friends and then began to call me out.

"What's up now? Talk that shit you was talking now Bitch!" She challenged while fake running up to me, swinging her fist and waiting for someone to hold her back. From that incident, I noted she was like most bullies or dogs with loud barks, all talk and no bite. I decided that if an audience is what she wanted then an audience is what I was going to provide her with.

I made my way to the lunchroom and briefed Principal Vapor on what was happening and what my plan was for handling it. I told her that on Friday, I was going to fight Olivia after school. Principal Vapor did not object to my reasoning and informed me that I should be prepared for a three day suspension after the fight. She told me that because Olivia was 18, she would be expelled from school.

The current day was Wednesday and I began to spread the word around school so we could form an audience for the fight. For the remainder of the week, I didn't have any issues from her. She ignored me in the hallways and all bullying from her friends ceased. I thought about calling the fight off, but I felt like I was already in too deep. I'd rallied up five friends that didn't attend our school to meet me there on Friday, just in case they planned on jumping me. My friends were extremely excited and looked forward to it like it was the Oscar De La Hoya vs Félix Trinidad fight. I didn't want to let them down.

After school on Friday, I followed Olivia outside and patiently waited as she said her goodbyes to her friends that seemingly knew what was going on, but didn't want any parts of the drama. My five friends were at the corner of the building when they spotted me and loudly probed, "Where that Bitch at?"

"She's right here!" I deeply vocalized, confirming to Olivia that it was about to go down. Just then, a car pulled up in front of the building and Olivia unexpectedly hopped in on the passenger side.

"Bridgett, you got a problem with my daughter?" The driver, who was obviously her mother, quizzed.

"Your daughter has a problem with me and I don't even know why!" I informed her in a polite manner, being that my mama didn't play when it came to respecting elders.

"Bitch ain't nobody got no problem with your bald headed ass!" Olivia shot back from the safety of the passenger seat.

"Get out of the car and I'ma show you who the Bitch is!" I threatened.

"You better get out and beat her ass!" Olivia's mother ordered.

She stepped out of the car and slowly began to take her jacket off. The audience of classmates were hooting and hollering, "Hit her Bridgett! Just hit her!"

I wanted to ensure that it was a fair fight and announced to the crowd, "Nah, I'ma let her get her jacket off first!" It took her forever to get that jacket off. Presumably, she was stalling in hopes that someone was going to step in and put a stop to the Friday night after school entertainment.

As soon as her jacket hit the ground, I hit her with the jab, cross, jab, cross, right hook, left hook combination that I'd been studying for the occasion. That last hook landed on her eye and left her stumbling and looking for something to rest upon.

"Get out and help your sister!" Olivia's mom ordered her younger daughter to get out of the car and fight me as well. Her sister came flying out of the back seat like a shooting star. I was forced to think quickly and hit lil sis with a repeated jab, cross combination until one of my five friends ran over to help me out. My girl took on the sister just as Olivia caught her balance and rejoined me in the fight.

The security guards finally came and broke up the commotion as the students were going wild. I was so empowered by the adrenaline that I broke away from the guard's choke hold and swiftly ran down the street with my friends to the getaway cars! I already knew I was going to get suspended for three days but they would have to inform me by telephone because I was out of there.

The six of us sped off, three in one car and three in another. We were laughing, cheering and hi-fiving one another as we recklessly drove to our next destination, The Desoto Bass Projects aka The Bass. When we got to the projects, we were hanging out of the windows boasting about our triumph over the fight and daring anybody to mess with us and we'd beat them up too. We felt good, dominant and invincible until a car pulled up to us with four unknown dudes inside of it.

"Aye, y'all can't be over here bringing all that drama and noise this way. Gone somewhere else with all that." The passenger suggested.

"Who the hell do you think you are with your punk ass? This is a free country and we can do whatever we please. You ain't the police!" My feisty friend shot back and the rest of us agreed.

"Oh yeah? That's how you feel?" The driver responded. "Let's show these porch monkey's how we get down in The Bass!" He ordered his passengers.

The dude in the backseat rolled his window down, just as the driver began pressing on his accelerator while the car was in park, causing his tires to spin in place, leaving a thick cloud of smoke all around us. The dude in the back seat then picked up a shotgun and pointed it in our direction. The six of us screamed loud enough to drown out our dopamine of courage and ducked down to take cover in anticipation of the cars getting shot up.

"Scary ass bitches!" The driver yelled out as the rest of the boys guffawed at our extreme trepidation. At that point, he burned more rubber with his tires then sped off down the street, leaving us in an emotional upheaval with lungs full of exhaust pipe smoke. Grateful they didn't make us meet our maker, we concluded it was time for us to get off the streets and into our respective homes.

After the encounter with them boys from The Bass, I was struck with an attitude of gratitude like many people develop after a near death experience. Feelings of guilt and sorrow burdened me for what I'd done to Olivia. I still had no idea what we were even beefing over so I decided I would apologize and present her with a truce once we crossed paths again.

After my three day suspension, Principal Vapor came and forcefully withdrew me from class like I'd done something wrong. "Come with me, Ms. Hatch!" She demanded, pulling me up from my desk by the arm.

"Ouch, you're hurting me!" I over dramatized. "I didn't do nothing, I swear!" She escorted me into an empty classroom and informed me about what had transpired. Olivia, her sister and their mother were at the school looking to gang up and beat me down. Because they couldn't find me, the three of them jumped on the closest person to me that they could find, my friend Latrice. She was innocent and didn't have anything to do with the drama. I was heated and the desire to make amends with them went right out the door.

"Oh hell nah, I got to get over there!" I attempted to run out of the room but the door wouldn't budge. Principal Vapor had locked me inside and wouldn't allow me to leave. Tears of frustration rolled down my puffy cheeks as I was ready to avenge my friend's misfortune. "Please let me out of here!" I banged at the door.

"No, Ms. Hatch. This is going to have to play out without any further involvement by you. If you do retaliate, I will expel you right along with Olivia and you will not graduate. Do you understand me?" She declared.

"Ok! I hear you. Dang!" I agreed. Olivia was already expelled from the school just like Principal Vapor predicted but her sister got an additional ten day suspension for their counterattack. I'm not sure as to what happened with their mother and if charges were pressed on her for ambushing a minor or not. The sister and I continued to attend school together without any further incident but Latrice got transferred to another school. Her mom felt the school was in the wrong for suspending her when she'd only fought to defend herself. I concur. It wasn't fair but unless I was willing to flunk out of school, there was nothing I could do about it.

Weeks later, I was kicking it with my homegirls Carly and Daisha, two of the five friends that showed up to fight with me that day. We went to the drive-through store where we knew we wouldn't get carded and purchased some Seagram's Gin and Juice, Newport cigarettes and Grape Swisher Sweet cigars to prepare for our little gathering at Daisha's house.

As expected, the weed had us acting all goofy, cracking jokes on one another and blurting out silly ideas.

The alcohol had us feeling loose, clumsy and slurring our speech. Carly was holding on to the blunt while reading her book and laughing hysterically at something she'd read in it. "Puff Puff pass hoe!" Daisha enforced the general unspoken rule of the art of smoking with friends. Everyone knows you're supposed to hit the blunt a couple times, then pass it to the next person in rotation.

Carly was too busy reading her book that she didn't hear Daisha and therefore continued to violate the law. Daisha went into a full out party of one, joke cracking session! "You ole bubble gum, lemon drop, water head, Dora The Explorer looking ass! Pass the blunt with yo Swiper no swiping, blunt hogging ass!"

The fact that she referenced a cartoon show, Dora The Explorer, had me laughing uncontrollably in derision! I was laughing so hard that I fell off the couch and right on to the glass that I was drinking my alcohol out of. The impact of my knee hitting the glass caused it to shatter and a piece was lodged into my right knee cap. "Hahahaha look, I'm bleeding but I can't feel the pain!" I chuckled. Daisha came to my rescue by pulling the glass out and stopping the bleeding with a paper towel while Carly still puffed on the blunt.

"Aye, y'all know where we should go like right now, right now?" Carly quizzed.

"Bitch, we need to go to the hospital so my ass can get some stitches!" I continued to convulse with laughter while holding the blood drenched paper towel in the air, revealing the massive amount of blood being lost.

"Nah, not no damn hospital! We should go get some tattoo's!" She whispered like there was someone in the room she didn't want to share her elaborate plan with.

"Hell yeah let's get some tattoos!" Daisha seconded.

Finally coming down off my laughing high, I grabbed a t-shirt and applied pressure to the laceration on my knee until the bleeding finally stopped. "Why we still sitting here then? Let's go!" I consented. Daisha wrapped my knee with gauze and an ace bandage she'd found in the medicine cabinet, then we set out to the nearest tattoo parlor.

We searched through the mountain of tattoo picture books for ideas. Daisha's eyes were drawn to a baby panda bear that she got tatted on one of her boobs. Carly got excited when she saw a Lion, her high school's mascot and tatted it on her arm along with c/o 99, representing the year she graduated. My heart landed on a pair of boxing gloves, believing I'd exhibited the skills in that high school fight. I didn't have enough heart to get such a huge piece of work and deliberately settled for the smallest tattoo I could find; a flower with a leaf on each side and my nickname, BOO underneath it.

Following the drunken stupor of three teenagers permanently marking our bodies, we headed back to Daisha's house to get the party started all over again. I then got a call from my friend Latrice informing me that she was over at my house with my mama, brother and sister. She stopped by to hang out, thinking I would be there. I promised I was going to hop on the next RTA bus and would be on my way home.

By the time I made it to the bus stop, strong winds, heavy rain and rapid flash lightning was followed by an immense acoustic effect on the earth's atmosphere; authoritative thunder. I was caught smack dab in the middle of a severe thunderstorm! Unlike most, I absolutely love thunder and rain for all it does for the earth as well as the serene, tranquil and meditative frame of mind it yields for me when blessed with its presence. I didn't mind being within the confines of the storm.

Latrice and my family were at the kitchen table playing cards when I walked in. I stood at the door so they could get a good look at my disheveled appearance that stole their attention. My hair was soaked, wet and covering the sour look on my face. My clothes were dripping wet, leaking all over the living room carpet and my breathing was shallow. Everyone's eyes went directly to my ace bandaged right knee and the gauze taped on my right arm. I looked like a patient who was just discharged from the hospital against medical advice.

"What the hell happened to you?" Mama screeched. I continued to stand there quietly, disregarding her question in order to make the moment more dramatic. "Girl have you lost your damn mind? What you done got yourself into?" Mama asked for the second time as she stood up from the table. I knew I'd better answer her if I didn't want to get knocked into next week. She didn't like to repeat herself!

"I got struck by lightning!" I wailed with the most believable cry I could summon at the time.

"Oh my God! Are you ok? Come here, let me take a look at it!" Mama worried.

"She's lying Ms. Donella! She ain't get struck by no lightning! She done went and got a tattoo!" Latrice squealed while chuckling so hard that slobber was running down the corner of her mouth as she bent over, slapping herself on the knee.

"Let me see! Take those bandages off!" Mama ordered. I obeyed and unwrapped my right knee revealing the now swollen and open laceration.

"I fell on top of a glass at Daisha's house." I confessed before Mama could get a word out, hoping that would soften the blow when I revealed that Latrice was correct in her assumption.

"We should go to the hospital and get this stitched up so it doesn't leave a nasty scar." Mama lovingly offered.

"Nah, it'll be alright." I declined, thinking I knew best. The nasty scar wouldn't still be visible on my right knee to this day had I listened to Mama.

"What about your arm?" Latrice was determined to prove she was right.

"Ok! Ok! You got me!" I removed the gauze and revealed the minuscule work of art.

"I knew it! You can't fool me!" Latrice exclaimed as my sister Deya shook her head with signs of discord.

"Have you lost your damn mind?" Mama inquired. "What does that even say? I can barely see it." She grabbed my arm, bringing it closer to her while squinting her eyes. "800?"

"No, it says BOO, the nickname you gave me." I said in a sweet tone, hoping she'd find it to be a loving and sentimental gesture and not slap the black off of me!

"Well, it's your body I guess. You the one have to go around for the rest of your life with ink all over you." Her tone softened and I knew I got her with that last statement.

"I almost got a pair of boxing gloves tatted on my face! Y'all know I think I'm Tyson!" I joked.

"Then I really would have laid you out with that jab, cross, jab, cross combination you think you know so well!" Mama kidded. We all laughed at the fact that I thought I was some type of professional fighter after getting into only one real fight. What I didn't know was that I'd be fighting many more battles in the near future.

Do you find yourself fighting others either physically or verbally quite often? If so, know that your fighting spirit isn't a bad or negative characteristic. You were born to fight. You just might be fighting the wrong battles. This may be the perfect time for you to assess your stance and get your fight in order.

The battles you take on is a testament to your character. History gives us many great examples of others who knew what their mission was and had their fight in order. Whether it was Marcus Garvey fighting to unify and connect people of African descent, Mike Tyson fighting competitively as a professional boxer or Jesus fighting for the salvation of the world, each of them fought according to their life's purpose and couldn't be swayed otherwise.

To all my fellow fighters out there, God drafted you as a fighter. Your responsibility is to fuel your fight with the fruits of the spirit which are love, joy, peace, patience, kindness, goodness, faithfulness, gentleness and self-control. If you're not sure, you can pray and ask God how to best use your fighting spirit to reveal your mission in life. There's an old African proverb that says, *"A warrior fights with courage, not with anger."* Ask yourself, how am I fighting?

"The Lord will fight for you; you need only to be still."
Exodus 14:14 NIV

Scotiart by Scot Schneir

"Vibrations"

Los Angeles, CA

Chapter 9: What Now
Smarty Pants

The fervently anticipated day had finally come, May 31, 2000! By the time the average student reached high school, they had three prior graduations; kindergarten, elementary and junior high. I wasn't afforded that luxury as I was merely assigned to the next levels of education and couldn't participate in the graduation ceremony due to my poor grades, attendance and behavior. I was so elated to be included in the celebration that I wrote myself a message that morning on a "thank you" card. It read:

Dear Bridgett LaRé Hatch,

Thank you for getting yourself out of school and making the first step to success. No one thought you would be a high school graduate but you showed all them ignorant fools. You Did It! Not all by yourself but by God's grace. So I thank God for being with me through it all. I owe it all to Him and of course my mom.

Love, Boo % 2000

The fact that I walked down that stage at The Memorial Hall and accepted my high school diploma was a huge shock to my friends, family, teachers and myself alike. It was no surprise how excited my dad was in the car after the ceremony while driving my friends and I home. "Bridge, I'm so proud of you! Here's your card and a little something, something for you!" I opened the "Congratulations Class of 2000 Graduate" card that disclosed two new, crispy $20 bills inserted inside.

"Awww, thank you. That was sweet." I stated in an ungrateful and dry manner after reading the card.

"You're welcome Daughter! What are you going to do with your tassel? You should give it to me so I can hang it in my rear view mirror!" Dad suggested, clearly missing the sarcasm in my response.

"Give you my tassel? Now why in the hell would I do that? You ain't done shit to help me get here and now you want an award? If anybody gets this tassel, it'll be my mama, not you with your Wild Irish Rose drinking ass!" As the words escaped from my tongue, I couldn't believe I was saying them, but it was too late to draw back.

There was only one other time I'd talked to my dad with such disrespect. One day, he and his girlfriend who was pregnant with twins, took me to get my hair braided. As soon as my dad walked into the braiders home, which I admit was a bit unkempt, he went off on her and everybody else in the house. "This nasty as hell! I'm not leaving my daughter in this dirty ass house. You need to get up off your butt and clean this shit up before you have people come over here! Come on Bridge, let's go!" He insisted as he walked back to the car.

Not invested in what the lady's house looked like and only wanting to get my hair done, I immediately called Mama and brought her up to speed. She instructed me to repeat after her, "I hope y'all get into a car wreck and die!" I obeyed and Dad left me there to fend for myself.

So there we were in the car after my graduation and I'd cursed him out yet again, but this time, on my own accord. Dad pulled the car over and looked in the backseat. My friend Harmony's toddler son was playing with his army soldier. "If she didn't have this child with her, I'd put all y'all asses out my car!" He assured me.

"Whatever! Just drop us off so I can give this little punk ass $40 to the weed man real quick!" I continued with the dishonor as my friends looked on in utter disbelief while Dad blasted the radio to drown me out.

I can only assume the sudden burst of rage stemmed from feeling entitled to more than what he had to offer the entire duration of my childhood. Wanting him to fit into my box of what I conceived a dad should be, I didn't understand that he did the best he could with what he had and knew. Him and Mama both for that matter. I just needed more from them and didn't have the knowledge, courage or words to articulate myself well. My expression of hurt seeped out in the only way I felt comfortable with, anger.

Can you relate to being unappreciative of the people God placed in your life that has contributed to any success you may enjoy today? They may not have contributed in a way that you saw fit, nonetheless, it was God's will. If so, you may want to consider partaking in this gratitude exercise given to my clients in The BRIDGE Method. It's a transformational program designed to equip you with tools, techniques and exercises to bridge the gap from playing small to being in the fullness of your truth. For more information about The BRIDGE Method, go to www.bridgettlare.com.

Here's how the Gratitude Exercise works... Secure a notebook and pen to create a list of at least 25 people who have added value to your life. Consider both the people who are positive as well as negative. Think of these people without any judgement on their character, only the value they've added that provoked a positive change in you. For example, my dad wasn't emotionally available due to his lifestyle choices. The value he added to my life is the drive and passion for transformation and a mission to help others heal from past traumas.

Once you have your list of 25 names, ask yourself, "Have I ever told them how grateful I am for what they've done for me?" For every person you answer no to, write a handwritten thank you note and deliver it to them. This exercise was created to replace grudges, resentment or frustration with gratitude.

Now, where did I leave off in the story? Oh yeah, I remember... I was talking about cursing my dad out for adding value to my life. He quickly forgave me and bought my first car a few months later! Actually, it was more like I coerced him into getting a car for me. I'd found a 1995 two door, candy apple red Ford Thunderbird at a car lot in Middletown, about a half hour away. After being informed that I needed a $800 down payment, I promised the salesman that I'd be back for the car the next day.

For as long as I could remember, Dad had promised to buy me a car for my Sweet 16th. Instead of a car, he gave me three new siblings; a pair of twin sisters from his girlfriend and a baby brother from another mother. He pinpointed his new responsibilities as the reason I couldn't get what I so desperately wanted. I devised a plan that would force him to keep his word and immediately called him to put the scheme in motion. "Hello Daughter!" He answered.

"Hey there! I found a car in Middletown and need you to drive me there to pick it up tomorrow. Can you take me?" I inquired in an honest and loving tone.

"You already got the money to buy it right?" He questioned apprehensively.

"I'm going to finance it. I was already approved and everything." I stated, disclosing only half of the truth.

The next day at the dealership, I signed all the papers with Dad proudly standing by my side when the salesman asked for the $800 down payment to close the deal. "$800? I didn't know I had to give you any money today!" I responded as shocked and appalled as I could be. "I don't have any money on me until I get paid next week. Do you think you can spot me?" I looked over at my Dad who was rubbing his head in frustration, yet none the wiser.

"I can write you a check but you have to be sure to pay me back next week." He looked into my eyes, ensuring I understood the seriousness of his request.

"Thank you! You'll be the first to know as soon as I get my check!" I misguided him, rationalizing that he indeed owed me. I quickly learned that God meant business when he instructed us to honor our mother and father!   Karma swiftly entangled itself into this situation in the months that followed.

I couldn't hold down a job long enough to keep up with my car payments and afford the party girl lifestyle that I was accustomed to. I went from one customer service to telemarketing job after another. The fact that I type over 90wpm due to being a business major in high school was a blessing and a curse. I knew the moment I got fired or quit one job that it wouldn't be long before I got another elsewhere because of my exceptional administrative skills. In my lifetime, I have been hired, fired and dragged out by security from so many jobs that I lost count once it reached 100!

Besides stealing, most of the reasons I quit or got fired were unnecessary and could have been prevented but immaturity and ego combined was a self-destructive combination. I remember working as a telemarketer for a magazine subscription company. We had a team meeting one morning and someone was holding a side conversation as the supervisor was speaking. Being that I was usually the one with the blabbermouth, the supervisor assumed I was the guilty party. "Bridgett, you need not to talk when I'm talking." She asserted.

"Excuse you but that wasn't even me." I shot back.

"Well it sounds a lot like you."

"Well it wasn't. Man, you tripping!" I nonchalantly stated.

"You don't tell your boss she's tripping!" She raised her tone of voice, shocked and irritated by me challenging her assumption.

"Stop tripping then!" I continued in a low tone, still high and relaxed from my morning blunt.

"You know what? That's it! You're out of here! I've had just about enough of your sassy mouth!" She pointed at the door, ordering me to leave.

I was infuriated because I was actually innocent but couldn't find the words to state my case, therefore, anger sufficed. Silent tears began to escape from my eyes and my mouth took on a mind of its own. "Bitch, who gone make me leave? Touch me and see what happens! I dare you!" I threatened with opened arms, welcoming her into my space.

The supervisor picked up the phone, "Security, please escort Bridgett out of the building and make sure she collects all of her belongings." She looked in my direction, "I bet you don't talk to another boss like that ever again in your life!"

"Boss? Ain't nobody the boss of me! Your title is supervisor, that's all that you are!" I carried on until security made their way to the conference room to escort me out. "That's your problem. You feeling yourself way too much thinking you're the boss of somebody!"

"You can kiss your job goodbye and your last check will be mailed to you!" The supervisor asserted as I gathered my belongings from the desk.

"Do you know what you can kiss?" I pulled my pants down, exposed my back side and gave it a loud and hard slap. "My black ass!" The security officer grabbed me by the arm, forcefully removing me from the call center. I screamed loud enough for the customers on the phone to hear me, "Don't buy any magazines from this company. It's all a scam!" I lied as the door hit me where the good Lord split me.

At the time, that type of behavior was totally normal and justified to me because that's what was exhibited in the environment I was raised in. Instead of seeking gainful employment, I developed a new skill, switching price tags at Wal-Mart and paying ridiculously low prices for the higher priced items. I would then return the products in exchange for a gift card at the retail price and use them to keep gas in my car for the night clubs.

Remember when I earlier stated that karma swiftly entangled itself into the car scheme I ran on my dad? Well, one day I was at home getting ready for the club, ironing clothes and rapping along with my favorite old school song by Salt N Pepa...

"If I wanna take a guy home with me tonight,

it's none of your business,

and if she wanna be a freak and sell it on the weekend,

it's none of your business,

now you shouldn't even get into who I'm giving skins to,

It's none of your business,

so don't try to change my mind, I tell you one more time,

it's none of your business!"

In the middle of my jam session, Reggie came home and was genuinely startled to see me there. "I thought you left. Who's driving your car?" He asked.

"What do you mean who's driving my car? I'm clearly standing right here so apparently I haven't left yet!" I responded, annoyed by his disturbance.

"Well your car just left, smart ass!" He chuckled.

"What are you talking about, my car just left?" I ran outside and was met by nothing but asphalt where my car once reserved space. "Oh my God! Somebody stole my car!" I screamed and immediately called the police to report the vehicle stolen. The police asked me a number of questions like do I make payments and am I behind on said payments. After answering yes to both questions, the officer suggested I call the dealership to see if they had repossessed my car.

"Repossessed?" What is that? I asked the officer, never having heard the term before.

"It's when you miss a number of payments on your car loan and the dealership comes and takes their property back from you." He informed me.

"Is it legal?" I inquired, totally ignorant to what had transpired.

"Yes it's legal and there's nothing we can do about it. You have to contact the dealership and make arrangements to pay.

The police led me to the culprits that stole my car, the dealership. Being that I didn't have a job or money, I had no intentions on paying them and concocted a plan to retrieve my property back. I called DeNora and requested for her to pick me up around midnight and drive me to Middletown so I could repossess my car back.

Without hesitation, she showed up with her five-year-old daughter. Once we arrived at the dealership, I spotted my car and appointed DeNora's daughter to walk over with me and act as my lookout person. Just as I was about to unlock the door, her little voice whispered, "Here comes the police!" I looked around and spotted a cruiser driving down the alley with their lights off.

Whether someone saw us lurking and called the police, we tripped the alarm, or they weren't even on to me, I had no interest in sticking around to find out. "Oh shit! Let's get out of here!" I picked my little cousin up and hurriedly ran to DeNora's car, encouraging her to speed off. We fled the scene safely without any further incident and I chugged the repossession of my car up as a loss.

An overpowering air of melancholy began to dominate my life. There I was with no job, no money, no car and no plans for the future. My sister Deya attended Sinclair Community College where she received financial aid checks. In an attempt to convince me to accompany her, she showed me one of the quarterly checks received. I was easily convinced and enrolled within a week.

Not knowing what to major in, I chose criminal justice being that my dad, who was a corrections officer and my auntie, who was a police sergeant, were the only two people I knew in life with a career at that time. I started attending college and the checks started rolling in! All of my money went to clothes, alcohol, drugs and partying.

Hitting the club scene and balancing school was my full-time job, then the most remarkable thing happened. I surprisingly developed an appreciation for learning! I looked forward to attending classes, reading and doing research projects. On drunken nights that turned into drunken mornings, I still went to school unrested, reeking of booze and weed with skimpy club clothes on. I was all in.

Although committed to attending college, the indecisiveness about what the future held was weighing heavily on my chest. I switched my major almost every quarter. I went from criminal justice to psychology to political science and so on. Realizing that my life was going nowhere, I desired to make a positive change and have clear direction but I didn't know where to start. Can you relate? Do you ever feel like you're spinning in circles and not making any progress, stuck in indecision? If I can offer a suggestion, pray and ask God to show you the way, then do your part. Feel free to pray this following prayer…

"Show me the right path, O Lord; point out the road for me to follow. Lead me by your truth and teach me, for you are the God who saves me. All day long I put my hope in you. Psalm 25:4-5 NLT

After you pray, trust and believe that the will of God will be done and then stay in action because faith without work is dead. Find someone that's living a life that you desire to live, someone you admire. Take that person to lunch or somewhere and pick their brain. Ask open-ended, empowering questions. If you get answers that resonate with you, utilize the feedback and formulate a plan that best suits you.

You do not have to reinvent the wheel, Use the blueprint others have designed, add your own twist and make it yours. If you do not have anyone within reach to possibly learn from, you can invest in a life coach, therapist or mentor. A celebrity will suffice as well. Do your research by reading books, attending seminars and taking yourself through "Youtube University" where you can learn how to do or be anything you decide by simply learning from Youtube videos. Bottom line, create your own opportunities by using the resources that are readily available to you.   Like Pastor T.D. Jakes put it so beautifully, *"If you can't figure out your purpose, figure out your passion. For your passion will lead you right into your purpose."*

"The Lord says, "I will guide you along the best pathway for your life. I will advise you and watch over you. Do not be like a senseless horse or mule that needs a bit and bridle to keep it under control." Psalm 32:8-9 NLT

Roland Hatch Photography

"Stepping Stones"

Dayton, OH

Chapter 10: Bad Girl Gone Good

Genevive's invitation to attend Bible Study at Revival Center Ministries International couldn't have come at a better time. I'd been seeking purpose and truth. Although I didn't have a close relationship with God, I knew the timing of this invite was a divine intervention, so I accepted the offer.

Already in student mode from attending college, I paid close attention and took immaculate notes at church that day. The pastor said something about salvation and how it was for everybody, no matter what you have done in life. He said God loves me just the way I am and wanted to be in relationship with me.

Every word preached felt as if it was directed at me. Have you ever felt that way, like the pastor had zeroed in on you? My heart was vulnerable, heavy and mortified with conviction. I was looking for a way out of that state of being. "Is there anybody in here tonight that wants to give their life to God?" The pastor questioned the congregation and many of them proceeded to make their way to the altar, including Genevive. She motioned for me to join her, but I smirked and shook my head, no. The choir continued to sing, "We Fall Down" by Donnie McClurkin:

> *We fall down but we get up,*
> *We fall down but we get up,*
> *We fall down but we get up,*
> *For a saint is just a sinner who fell down and got up!*

"Your soul needs to be healed by the power of the living God." The pastor continued the altar call above the choir's melodic tunes. "If you don't know Jesus Christ as your Lord and Savior, come! I feel like it's one more person that God is calling on today." The pastor went on in a soft, loving, sing- song tone as I searched the crowd to see who that one more person was going to be.

I wasn't sure if it was the manipulation of the music or if I was the one more person the pastor spoke of but I began to softly whimper allowing a tear to escape my eye. I had a sudden urge to walk to the altar, but was afraid that I didn't know what to expect. "Come! God is calling for you. Don't look around or worry about what your neighbor is doing. If you feel it in your spirit that God is calling you then now is the time to answer the call. Come!" The pastor shouted.

I squeamishly stepped out into the aisle and slowly made my way to the altar. "There we go! Come as you are, says the Lord!" The pastor announced then placed the microphone to my mouth. "What's your name young lady?"

"Bridgett." I responded, sniffing up the tears that drained into my nose.

"Bridgett are you ready to accept the Lord as your Savior?"

"Ummm...Yes."

"Do you believe He died for you?"

"Ummm...Yes."

"Alright Church, everyone repeat after me." The pastor asserted as the church and myself awaited directions. "Lord Jesus, I come to you as a sinner, I lost my way but I know that you have the power to heal. I receive you right now into my life. Save me. Wash me. Cleanse me and renew me in the name of Jesus. Lord, I'm sorry for all my sins and I'm thankful that your blood washes my sins away. I give you all the glory, honor and praises. In Jesus name, Amen."

Not wanting to lie to the pastor, I committed to taking my new found salvation seriously. I made a conscious decision to become a woman of substance and took on the characteristics of a nun. By the grace of God, I developed the willpower to stop cursing, clubbing, stealing, lying, having sex, drinking alcohol and smoking weed. Some would have said I was more like the religious extreme of a nuisance.

We couldn't have a conversation without me trying to convince you that your life was in shambles and you were going to Hell. I would shove salvation and revelation videos in everyone's face in an attempt to persuade them to give their lives to God, repelling friends, family and strangers alike. Although, my strategy did seem to work really well with the men I would meet. Instead of a date, I'd invite them to church. On any given Sunday or Wednesday, I would bring different men with me, some of whom gave their lives to the Lord, even if it was just for that day.

The older women began to take notice of my plethora of new friends. I would hear the whispering and see the, "she ought to be ashamed of herself", looks they shared when I walked in. At first it was just an assumption until one of the women actually had the nerve to soothe her curiosity when she caught me by myself. "I see you don't have any of your guests with you today." She observed.

"Nope. Not today. Just me, myself and I." I respectfully stated.

"Who are those men that you bring with you anyhow?" She pried.

"Friends." I answered in a deadpan tone of voice.

"Un. Well how old are you anyways Baby?" Her voice seemed to turn from cold and judgy to loving and concerned.

"I'm Nineteen." I disclosed, using the same energy she gave me.

"Nineteen!" You only nineteen? Oh you should be over in the youth church services with the rest of the kids! Why don't you gone and check it out today?"

"Kids church?" I replied, suddenly feeling offended. "I'm too old to be going to some youth service?"

"Nah Baby, there are other nineteen, twenty and twenty-one year-olds in there right now. Gone and check it out for yourself. If you don't like it, then come on back out here with us." The Mother suggested.

I took her up on the offer and was initially happy that I did. The youth church was so much fun! The youth pastor looked to be only a few years older than I was. He was very knowledgeable of The Bible and made the lessons much more fun than they did in the adult services.

From that day forward, I attended the youth services by myself after deeming it inappropriate to invite grown men to join me there. I lived a few blocks from the church on Tyson Ave. and had to walk to and from church due to the car repossession situation. The walk wasn't unbearable, nonetheless, one of the youth members became aware of my circumstances and generously offered to carpool with me.

The carpool picked me up for the first time and I was very excited about building closer friendships with the kids that way. We got to church and the pastor announced we would be playing a competitive game. Excitement filled the room as we patiently awaited instructions.

"Alright y'all. We are going to play a game that rewards your teamwork abilities as well as organization skills." The youth pastor announced and continued, "I'm going to split you all up into two groups. Whichever group can line up the fastest in the order of your street name, wins the game! If your street name starts with an A then you're first and if it starts with a Z then you're last and everyone else is in between. Any questions?"

"No!" All of us youth members replied in unison.

"Alright! Get started on the count of three. One! Two! Three! Go!" The pastor exclaimed. Both groups were scrambling around and talking amongst ourselves, eager to beat the other team!

"Hurry! What does your street name start with?" The self-proclaimed leader of our group asserted.

"Um...My street name starts with a B!" I briskly answered as she forcefully positioned me third in line. Everyone behind me began to fall in order with ease under her direction.

"Finish!" Our self-proclaimed leader hollered as the other team continued to arrange themselves.

"Alright, now let's see if y'all know your alphabets or not!" The pastor joked. "Starting from the first person, go down the line and tell us your street name."

"My street name is Anna!" The first member said.

"My street name is Blairwood!" The next person called out.

"My street name is Boo!" I proudly stated.

"Hold up. Boo? There's a street name Boo in Dayton?" The pastor questioned. Suddenly, I realized the huge blunder I had made and pretended I didn't hear his question.

"I just picked you up from your house." The carpool driver admitted. "You live on Tyson." All eyes were on me, awaiting my response.

"Live? Oooooh you meant street name like the street you live on? I thought you meant my street name like what they call me in the streets!" I embarrassingly admitted.

"Oh my God! Are you kidding me? This is church, why would you have thought that?" The self-proclaimed leader of our group blurted out in utter disgust of my ignorance as the other group members joined in on her exhibition of dismay.

"What? Nobody else assumed he meant line up by the name they call you in the streets? No? Just me?" I tried to make light of the misunderstanding but no one was having it.

"Ok y'all. Game over! Settle down and let's get back to The Word." The pastor attempted to ease the tension in the room but my group continued to grumble as the other group laughed hysterically at my expense. That was the last day I attended youth services. I rationed that they were too immature for me when the fact of the matter was, I didn't feel like I fit in and isolated myself.

After going back to the adult church services, the overwhelming sensation of not belonging continuously crept in. Feeling like I wasn't hard enough for the streets or soft enough for church, I presumed myself to be an estranged alien, aimlessly wandering earth in search of my own kind, whomever that may be. I remembered my dad telling me that he went through a church phase when he graduated from high school. I welcomed the idea that what I was going through was just a phase as well.

I consciously worked on increasing my prayer life in an attempt to fight off the feeling of discontentment. My faith was ignited when my daily prayer for a car was answered in a way in which I would have never expected. My mama's friend purchased a used vehicle for her daughter but something transpired to where she freely gifted it to me. That was a sign that God heard my prayers and was rewarding me for being in school, going to church regularly and seeking a better life for myself.

After sharing my good news with Harmony, her response was, "Why does good stuff always happen to you?"

"Good stuff happens to who? Me?" I couldn't ascertain what she was talking about. As far as I was concerned, that was the only good thing that happened to me my entire teenage years. Now I understand that it's all about perspective. People on the outside looking in can recognize your blessings for what they truly are. Sometimes we are too distracted by our wants and desires to see clearly. As you read this book, I encourage you to stop for a moment and think of at least five situations that have proven to be a blessing in your life. Write down those five situations that you once thought were mediocre and meditate on how they have been a blessing to you.

I contemplated the reasoning as to why Harmony would say such a thing. After looking at my life through her lens, I realized she was right. She saw me graduate from high school against all odds. She heard the story of me cheating death as an infant. She knew about the drug dealers I took to the church who gave me money, asking for nothing in return and saw all of that as a good thing. Good stuff was always happening to me. It was often disguised as ratchetness or defeat but nonetheless, God used it for my good.

Once I began to connect the dots to all the good things that had happened in my life up until that moment, I started to like the person that I was for the first time in a long time. I held on to that feeling for as long as I possibly could, then my 20th birthday came around. Being that it was my first birthday as a good girl, I didn't quite know what to do or how to celebrate.

Knowing that I loved a good laugh, DeNora suggested we go to a comedy show. I was totally down for that until finding out it was at one of my old stomping grounds, The Majestic's Nightclub. "Girl you know I've done too much dirt at Majestic's. I don't need to be in nobody's club." I tried my luck in backing out of the comedy show.

"Girl! It's just a comedy show, not a club, club type of night. What trouble can you get into at a comedy show? Come on, it's your birthday!" She smirked.

"Well it has been a while since I been out anywhere. It is my birthday and I've changed. Ok, let's go!" I persuaded myself.

Many welcoming gestures were received from the same partygoers that frequented the clubs a year ago when I used to shut it down! The sense of belonging had returned.

We sat down at our table, awaiting the comedy show to begin when one of the street entrepreneurs that I would take to church came over. "What you doing in here?" He firmly stood above me with his arms crossed, genuinely interested in what my excuse could have been.

"Well it's my birthday and I like to laugh, soooo…" I begrudgingly shot back, resenting the fact that he was holding me accountable for the lifestyle I portrayed to him.

"You don't need to be in here. This ain't your type of scenery." He insisted.

"Boy, you don't even know the half of it. What you don't know is that before I started going to church and before I met you, I used to be in the club seven days a week. Trust me, I know how to handle myself." I ensured him.

Just then, the waitress walked up and asked for our food and drink orders. "Let them order whatever they want and put it on my tab." The young entrepreneur informed the waitress. "I still don't think you should be in here Boo." He stated his position one last time and walked away.

Initially, I only ordered food but was made aware of the two-drink minimum per person and felt obligated to order an alcohol beverage. "Um... I guess I'll have a Long Island Iced Tea." Never did it dawn on me to just get a Sprite!

"Hell yeah you will! It's your birthday!" DeNora screamed over the music, excitedly cheering me on with hi-fives. That one drink turned into two. Two drinks turned into three. Three drinks turned into me hitting a blunt with one of the fellow clubbers. The toxic patterns had returned at full tilt in one night of weakness. My 20th birthday marked the birth of a diabolical comeback.

I attempted to keep up with the church girl routine, school responsibilities and clubbing antics all at once. That proved to be much more than I wanted to bear. The church girl had lost the battle, bringing Dad's premonition that it was only a phase into fruition. The party girl was back with a vengeance. I'd succumbed to the bad girl lifestyle and went harder than ever before, especially after meeting a man who would challenge me to prove whether I was really about that life or not.

Genevieve and I both substituted church for hanging out in the projects a few blocks from our neighborhood where my cousin Yasmine lived with her son. We spent most days chilling on her porch, being entertained by the neighborhood dealers as they made their transactions. One day, we noticed a new guy in the neighborhood proceeding towards Yasmine's porch. "What's up Chocolate? How you doing?" The short, stalky, handsome dude with glasses addressed me.

"I'm chilling." I stated, trying to sound sexy and sultry but it came out raspy and choppy being that smoke was still in my lungs. I coughed to clear my throat. "Excuse me. What's up with you?"

"That blunt too much for your little lungs huh?" He joked. "What are you doing out here with these knuckleheads?"

"Oh I'm just chilling at my cousin's house for real. What's your name anyway? I never saw you around here." I remarked.

"Yeah because I got my own operation going on. My name "B" though. What's your's?" He inquired.

"What? They call me "B" as well. But my name is Boo. What a coincidence!" I exclaimed.

"Nah, ain't no such thing as coincidences, it's a match made in Heaven Baby." He smiled.

"It just might be!" I blushed. "Well does my Heavenly match have something better for me and my girls to do than to chill with these knuckleheads?"

"I got something for you to do for sure. Take my number and hit me up later. You won't regret it." He was mysterious and piqued my interest, so I took his number and later gave him a call.

The operation "B" spoke of was his own dope house which was on the same street I lived on, Tyson Ave. That house became my home away from home. On any given day, you could find, "B", myself, his homeboys and various drug users running in and out of the door.

After months of sitting in the dope house with him and hiding drugs on my person, the inevitable happened. Some thieves kicked in the back door, robbed and ransacked the place when it was unoccupied. The following day, I assisted him with cleaning up the spot and building a wooden barricade for the back door. "Boo, I'm going to need your help today so nobody thinks we're a joke over here okay?" He warned me.

"Okay what do you need me to do?" I questioned, eager to help.

"Just stick around, I need you to be here just in case these fools decide to come back. They won't think you're a threat."

"Um...well what is it that you need me to do exactly?" I nervously inquired.

"I'm not sure yet but when the time comes, I need to know that you got my back. Do you love me like you say you do?"

"You know I love you." I confirmed.

"Alright then that means you don't want nothing to happen to me, right?"

"Of course not! Whatever you need." I proclaimed.

He didn't have to try too hard to get me to do anything. "B" became yet another unmanageable, toxic addiction that I allowed to control and overpower me. It was like he could sense my insecurities, vulnerabilities and emotions and knew how to work me like a puppet. Later that day after cleaning the house up in preparation to reopen for business, "B" and I were cuddled up on the couch, smoking and watching music videos when someone knocked on the door.

"Who is it?" He yelled.

"What's up man, I just need to get a $20." The unknown drug user stated referring to a $20 piece of crack.

Just then, "B" reached under the couch, pulled out a handgun, inserted the magazine, cocked it back and handed it to me. "Hold this and point it at everyone that walks through the door, without saying a word." He demanded.

"What the hell? I'm not…"

"You love me don't you? Do you want someone to come in here and take me out or something?" He cut me off mid-sentence as the man grew impatient and began knocking on the door again.

"No." I answered while holding on to the gun.

"Go ahead and point it at the door and keep it on him until he leaves. You can do this Boo. Just look mean so these punks know you mean business. Let me see your mean face!" He joked, attempting to get a smile out of me.

"Open the damn door." I consented while holding the gun up towards the door, showing him my mean face.

"B" decided that it was time to promote me to a more meaningful position in his operation. I'd advanced from being the feminine energy at the dope spot to the unpaid gunman who just might shoot to kill on demand. Hindsight really is 20/20 and looking back, I can see how the 20-year-old me would have equated manipulation, guns and violence to love. Drama was my love language and "B" spoke it well.

Have you ever been overly nice, insecure or worried about what other people thought of you? If so, you may have been susceptible to manipulation which is a common human tactic. Psychological manipulation involves an attempt to control someone else and get them to do something to benefit the manipulator. These people look for and exploit others weaknesses. It works best on emotionally dependent individuals like children or those who are lost and seeking to find their place in life.

If you ever felt lost or feel lost now, know that there is hope. You don't have to have it all together but trust and believe that it will all come together for your good. The Bible says in Romans 8:28 KJV that, "...*all things work together for good to them that love God...*" Meditate and Pray on that scripture and believe it to be true for you.

Let's entertain for a moment, that losing yourself or struggling with opposition is how strength is built. If we didn't have any mess to dig through, how would we ever uncover our treasure? Losing yourself is how you find yourself, just like knowing what you don't want is how you learn what you do want.

It wasn't until the age of 33 that I considered not judging myself for the past. I began to get curious about my actions, then connected the dots. I can look back on these untamable teenage years to make sense of my story and ration why it was all imperative to becoming the woman I am today. You too may be judging yourself for your past or current circumstances. I am here to tell you to be encouraged. As long as you have breath in your body, there's room for transformation. You can and will achieve greatness if you decide to!

Allow yourself to fully explore on your journey of self-discovery to unlock who God created you to be, what you were created to do and the path you were created to take. The beauty of life is that it isn't linear. There's a lot of twists and turns to keep us engaged, otherwise, you may fall into a deep slumber, bored with the monotony and mediocrity of life. No matter where your path leads you, get the lesson, collect the treasure and enjoy the journey. There are far more journeys in life than there are destinations. On your journey, use your own discretion and don't allow anyone to do your thinking for you. Like Mama always says, *"You don't have to be mean, just say what you mean and mean what you say."*

"Your wickedness will punish you; your backsliding will rebuke you. Consider then and realize how evil and bitter it is for you when you forsake the Lord your God and have no awe of me," declares the Lord, the Lord Almighty. 20 "Long ago you broke off your yoke and tore off your bonds; you said, "I will not serve you!' Indeed, on every high hill and under every spreading tree you lay down as a prostitute. 21 I had planted you like a choice vine of sound and reliable stock. How then did you turn against me into a corrupt, wild vine?" Jeremiah 2:19-21 NIV

Marz Pacheco Original Art
"Un Patto Fatto" (A Pact Made)
Los Angeles, CA

About The Author

Bridgett is a self-proclaimed Reformed Bad Girl with a desire and mission to edify others to heal from past traumas and operate at the level of their fullest potential. She is not shy about her background of poverty, anger, promiscuity, drug and alcohol abuse. Bridgett provides tools for individuals who are ready to bridge the gap from playing small to living in the fullness of their truth with her transformational program, "The Bridge Method." She's an Award-Winning Speaker, Transformational Coach, Registered Nurse and International Best-Selling Author. Following an epiphany at the age of 33, Bridgett comprehended the fact that her current circumstances were far from what she wanted her legacy to be and sought after her true purpose. She's found purpose in helping others while transparently sharing the tumultuous stories of her fast life as a means to relinquish the bondage of shame, embarrassment and guilt in the world!

Mary Cruz Castillo

"Jeezus Series"

Los Angeles, CA